Creative Wire Jewelry

Ariella Nachshon

sixth&spring
books
New York, NY

sixth&spring
books

Copyright © 2011 by Sixth&Spring Books
161 Avenue of the Americas
New York, NY 10013
sixthandspringbooks.com

Produced for SOHO Publishing Company
by Penn Publishing Ltd.
www.penn.co.il

Editor: Shoshana Brickman
Design and layout: Michal & Dekel
Photography: Roee Feinburg
Styling: Roni Chen
Makeup artist: Perry Halfon

Library of Congress Cataloging-in-Publication Data

Nachshon, Ariella.
  Creative wire jewelry / by Ariella Nachshon. -- 1st ed.
     p. cm.
  ISBN 978-1-936096-11-4 (alk. paper)
  1. Wire jewelry. 2. Jewelry making. I. Title.
  TT212.N33 2010
  739.27'2--dc22
                                              2010040775

ISBN-13: 978-1-936096-11-4

Manufactured in China

1 3 5 7 9 10 8 6 4 2

First Edition

CONTENTS

INTRODUCTION

Joy and excitement filled me as I designed the projects for this book. It is my sincere wish that through these projects you will experience—and love—the colorful and creative world of making fashion jewelry and accessories.

Here I'll share with you, through many years of designing and making jewelry, my interpretation of working with wire. You'll find a wide variety of techniques, and be introduced to materials you might never have thought to use or combine. Some projects suggest color combinations that may seem unusual, showing you how the creative process transforms them into balanced pieces of jewelry that are harmonious and distinct.

So open the door to the limitless possibilities of wire jewelry. I'm sure you'll quickly discover how easy, rewarding and pleasurable it can be to make wonderful gifts—for yourself and for friends.

ACKNOWLEDGMENTS

More than a decade ago, there was a magical moment when I decided to follow my heart. I left my regular job and spread my wings. I chose to pursue self-fulfillment, and transformed my dream into reality. Though this road is challenging at times, the difficulties are nothing compared to the moments of exuberant happiness.

This book is a wonderful opportunity to thank the people who have supported and encouraged me along the way. First, I would like to thank Elan and Rachel for imagining this book, and for helping and supporting me through its development. I would like to thank my family, my husband, Nir, who has allowed me to follow my heart. To my wonderful children, Amiram, Yotam and Roni, who show an amazing amount of patience, even when the dining room table is full of beads. To my sister Shoshi and my friends Yael and Lori who are always there for me. Your presence in my life allows me to start every morning with a new creation.

This book is dedicated with love to my dear parents. To my mother, Dina, whose wisdom guides me wherever I go, and to my father Machluf, who cultivates my creativity through his own art.

USING THIS BOOK

Every project in this book is ranked according to skill level. These levels are meant to guide you in your project selection, but they shouldn't stop you from trying something out of your range.

Easy

★ ☆ ☆ ☆ If you are just starting to work with wire, these projects are right for you.

Intermediate

★ ★ ☆ ☆ These projects are perfect for readers with a bit of experience working with wire and making jewelry.

Advanced

★ ★ ★ ☆ These projects call for a variety of techniques.

Challenging

★ ★ ★ ★ These projects call for a variety of techniques and materials. They may be a bit more complex than the other projects.

MATERIALS

THE EXPERIENCE OF FINDING MATERIALS

Looking for and buying materials is an important part of the creative process. It can also be a genuinely fun experience! A rich variety of materials can be found all over the world (and on the Internet of course) to suit every style and budget.

In addition to looking for materials in bead shops and craft stores, I recommend checking out second-hand clothing stores, art and craft fairs, flea markets and wherever else you may find inspiration. In these out-of-the-ordinary places you're likely to find unusual elements such as old pieces of jewelry that can be taken apart and reused to make something entirely new and unique. Sometimes, my choice of materials starts from an idea or image that is already in my mind. Other times, the creative process is inspired by the material itself. For me, the most fascinating situation is seeing an item I like but not being sure what to do with it. I experiment with different ways of arranging it and all of a sudden—it happens! The item becomes a piece of jewelry, the result of my personal touch.

After you acquire the basic materials: jump rings, eye pins and clasps, the rest can be left to imagination and taste. The choice and combination of materials is what makes your jewelry distinct, what gives it your personal stamp.

WIRE

Working with wire can be challenging on both the creative and technical levels. Meeting these challenges is possible thanks to wire's wonderful trait of being flexible and malleable in the hands of the artist. The simplicity of wire and its clean appearance make it an excellent base for any creation, no matter how complex.

Wire can be used for stringing beads, wrapping components and creating a wide variety of shapes. Wire can be wrapped, twisted, twirled and bent. It can be the dominant element of a piece of jewelry, or it can be secondary to beads or other components that take center stage. I find that the more I work with wire, the more I realize how pleasant it is to work with and what endless possibilities it offers for creation.

The projects in this book make use of two main categories of wire: basic metal wire and precious metal wire. The basic type is metal wire (usually copper) with various coatings and colors. I recommend using this type of wire to develop your skills. Memory wire also falls into this category. It is coiled wire that holds its shape and is sold in a range of diameters suitable for making chains, bracelets and rings. The precious metal wire category includes sterling silver, gold-plated and gold-filled wire. These wires are wonderful to work with and produce beautiful results. They are more expensive than basic metal wire, so I recommend using them only after you have acquired skills by working with basic metal wires. Indeed, when you decide to make a project using precious metal wire, practice first with basic metal wire. This way, you'll know exactly how much precious metal wire to cut and be experienced in how to shape it. Both basic metal wires and precious metal wires are available in a range of thicknesses (measured in gauge), shapes and levels of hardness.

Gauge

Wire thickness is measured in gauge or mm: the lower the gauge, the thicker the wire. Here is a table to help you convert gauge measures to mm and inches.

GAUGE	MM	INCHES
14	1.5	0.06
16	1.3	0.05
18	1.0	0.04
20	0.8	0.03
22	0.6	0.03
24	0.5	0.02
26	0.4	0.02
28	0.3	0.01
32	0.2	0.008

Hardness

Wire is sold in three levels of hardness: soft, half-hard and hard. The projects in this book use half-hard or soft wire.

Shape

Wire may be round, half-round, square or twisted. All the projects in this book use round wire.

BEADS

Many of the projects in this book incorporate a few beads, some of them dozens. Beads add color and texture to wire jewelry, as well as a bit of a sparkle. While you can certainly use the beads I selected for these projects, feel free to make substitutions or alterations, adding or replacing beads according to your preference to create beaded wire jewelry that is entirely unique.

Acrylic beads

These beads are available in a large variety of shapes, textures and colors. Often made to imitate glass beads, crystals and gemstones, they are relatively light, an advantage in projects that require lots of beads.

Ceramic and porcelain beads

These decorative beads are often hand-painted and feature delicate patterns and motifs.

Cloisonné beads

These elegant enamel beads add a beautiful touch to any piece of jewelry. I recommend using them selectively, integrating a few with just the right combination of ordinary beads to highlight their beauty.

Crystal beads

These beads are very popular today, and with good reason. They fit well into so many types and styles of jewelry and add magnificent color and shine. Crystal beads come in a variety of sizes, shapes and finishes. Their quality and price also vary. I recommend Swarovski or Czech crystals for best variety and quality.

Czech pressed glass beads

This category encompasses beads in a variety of shapes, sizes and colors. It includes beads with leaf, heart and flower shapes, as well as beads with a variety of finishes. All are easy to find and come in a variety of prices. Foil glass beads are embedded with gold, silver or copper and are a rich addition to any piece of jewelry. Both of these bead types come in a wide range of prices.

Freshwater pearls

I love pearls. In particular, I love the distinct light that only pearls possess. Pearls not only add a classic touch to jewelry but also are quite trendy and worn by fashionable people of all ages. Pearls are much more affordable today than in the past and can be found in diverse sizes, shapes, colors and finishes.

Gemstones

These natural beads come in a limitless selection of sizes, shapes and colors. They are often polished, for added shine, but can also be found with natural finishes. Gemstones can upgrade the appearance of your jewelry, creating pieces you'll be delighted to wear for many years. The projects in this book feature a wide variety of gemstones, including turquoise, lapis lazuli, agate and aquamarine. It is possible (and sometimes preferable) to use imitation gemstones since they are considerably lighter than real ones.

Glass beads

A tremendous number of beads fall into this category. They come in countless shapes, colors and sizes.

Glass pearls

These pearly beads are actually glass beads coated with pearl color. They come in a wide range of uniform shapes, sizes and colors. If you select these beads for a project, make sure they are of high quality since you don't want the pearly coating to peel off over time.

Lampwork beads

Characterized by their vibrant colors and patterns, just a few lampwork beads can make a stunning piece of jewelry. Though they are traditionally handmade, factory-made copies are becoming increasingly available.

Metal beads

These beads may be coated with paint or left in their natural silver, gold or bronze color.

Metal-coated plastic beads

These beads look metallic but are actually metal-coated plastic. They are considerably lighter than regular metal beads, an advantage when making earrings or jewelry with lots of beads. Select high-quality beads of this type so that the metal finish doesn't chip off.

Murano and foil glass beads

Murano beads are handmade glass beads originating in the area of Venice, Italy. They are famed the world over for their high quality and beauty.

Seed beads

These common beads come in a vast array of shapes, colors, sizes and finishes. Japan is known for manufacturing high-quality seed beads that have standard-size holes for even the smallest beads. The system for measuring these beads is unique because the numbers are inversely proportional to the size; in other words, the larger the bead, the smaller the size number.

Shell and mother of pearl

These can add a natural element to wire jewelry. They come in a variety of textures and add a special brilliance.

Wire beads

These beads are made of coiled and twisted wire.

STRINGING MATERIALS

While wire is used as a stringing material in many of these projects, countless other stringing materials may be used to make jewelry.

Flexible silicone cord

Stretchy like a rubber band, this cord is suitable for making bracelets. In my experience, the optimal thickness is 0.032" (0.8 mm), which is strong enough to carry the weight of the bracelet and will fit into the holes of most beads. Silicon cord measuring 0.024" (0.6 mm) is suitable only for very small beads.

Lace, cord, thread and ribbon

These materials are excellent for making jewelry that includes knots, macramé or knitting. They are available in various colors, types, textures and thicknesses. Like all materials, they come in different levels of quality. I recommend investing in high-quality items that are strong and long-lasting.

Nylon thread

This is the most common type of thread used in jewelry making, and it comes in many thicknesses and colors. I generally use nylon thread that is 0.014" (0.35 mm) to 0.018" (0.45 mm) thick. Transparent thread is best, unless you want the color of the thread to be part of your jewelry (using blue nylon thread to string translucent beads, for example).

Nylon-coated steel beading wire

This is my favorite type of thread for jewelry making since it is easy to use, flexible, and comes in a variety of colors and thicknesses. It is durable over time and doesn't require a needle for stringing beads. The only drawback is that kinks can form if the wire isn't folded. When using this type of wire to string bracelets and chains, I recommend a diameter of 0.014" (0.35 mm) to 0.018" (0.45 mm). For heavier jewelry, I recommend wire that is 0.024" (0.60 mm) thick.

COMPONENTS AND OTHER MATERIALS

Bails

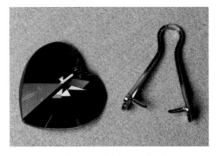 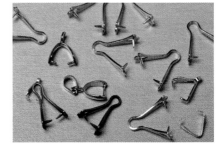

These can be used instead of jump rings to connect delicate charms to chains.

Bead caps

These metallic elements can be placed on either side of a bead to add richness and shine. They can also be strung with wide ends together for an unusual effect. Make sure you select bead caps that suit the size of your beads.

Bead tips

These are used to hide knots and crimp beads and connect clasps. They give jewelry a cleaner and more polished look. Like other jewelry components, these are available in a variety of materials and sizes. Select the bead tip according to the colors used in the project and the size of the item they are meant to conceal.

Buttons

Available in a variety of materials (including shell, wood, metal and glass), buttons add an interesting twist to jewelry and accessories.

Chains

These come in an endless variety of sizes and shapes. Some are made with basic metal, others with gold or silver. In this book, you'll see dozens of different chains and chain combinations.

Charms

These are used in many projects in this book, as a simple way of adding decoration (to a clasp, for example) or as a central element in the design. Metallic charms are often coated with silver, bronze or gold. Charms can also be made from top-drilled gemstones, crystals and glass beads by stringing a thin jump ring or bail through the hole.

Clasps

A wide variety of clasps are available for securing jewelry. Though traditionally positioned at the back of jewelry, clasps can also be placed at the side or front, adding a unique element to the composition and appearance. Consider this possibility when selecting clasps for your work.

Simple clasps Lobster claw clasps are the most common type of jewelry clasp. They are easy to use and usually located at the back of the item. They can also be used to connect accessories and are especially handy when you want to make an extension chain.

Special clasps A wide variety of decorative clasps are available today, among them multistrand box clasps, toggle clasps and hook-and-eye clasps. I recommend choosing a special clasp when you want it to be a visible part of the jewelry or your jewelry consists of several strands.

Connector bars

As their name suggests, these are used to connect parts of jewelry to each other or to the clasp. They come with any number of loops.

Cord tips and crimp ends

These accessories, affixed to the ends of chains, laces, threads and ribbons, allow you to connect clasps or pendants. They come in various sizes and have a loop at one end.

Crimp beads

These metallic beads are used to finish pieces of jewelry by securing the wire or thread you are stringing. They can also be used to position beads on string by flattening them at certain places along the stringing material. When selecting crimp beads, choose just the right size for the wire or lace you are using.

Earring findings

There are many options for finishing earrings: hook ear wires, leverback ear wires, ear posts and hoops (with or without loops), to name just a few. Chandelier and drop components are used to make decorative dangling earrings.

Hair combs and hair bands

These can be decorated with metal wire, beads and ribbon. They come in various colors and sizes.

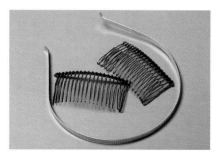

Jewelry adhesive

This is used to affix materials.

Jump rings

These small rings are essential for connecting elements when making jewelry. They are made from various materials and come in different gauges and sizes. I always have a variety on hand so that I can select the jump ring that is most appropriate for the project.

Soldered jump rings These cannot be opened. They are used when you need a secure connection.

Split rings These feature a double loop and cannot be opened. They can be strung onto string or other jump rings and help to ensure a very secure finish.

Unsoldered jump rings These can be opened and closed using two pliers.

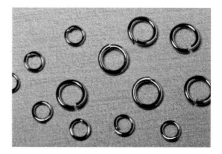

Pin backs

These flat-backed pins can be glued, sewn or secured with wire to make brooches.

Pins

These are made from basic or precious metals and come in various gauges and lengths. Make sure the pin gauge you choose is appropriate for your beads. Also check to make sure the pins are long enough for the beads you intend to string. Longer pins can be trimmed to size, but finding just the right size from the beginning cuts down on waste.

Eye pins These pins have a loop at one end. After stringing on beads, secure the other end with a loop.

Head pins These pins have a flat head at one end. After stringing on beads, secure the other end with a loop.

Plastic mesh tube

This marvelous material can be used to enclose beads to create an unusual effect. It comes in various colors and widths.

Ring base

Many (though not all) of the ring projects in this book require a premade base. Ring bases come in various styles, materials and sizes. I recommend buying high-quality ring bases that will hold up to regular wear.

Sketching materials

I often recommend sketching ideas before starting a project. Having pencils, a sharpener, an eraser and paper on hand makes this easy and convenient.

Spacer beads and bars

These may be used as a decorative element to separate beads or create symmetry and precision in a piece of jewelry.

Tassels	These ornaments are made from strands of chain, thread, yarn or satin. They add a playful, even musical element to your jewelry.

TOOLS

A NUMBER OF TOOLS ARE ESSENTIAL WHEN MAKING WIRE JEWELRY—THESE ARE THE TOOLS LISTED WITH EACH PROJECT. OTHER TOOLS AREN'T CRUCIAL BUT THEY CERTAINLY MAKE THE JEWELRY-MAKING PROCESS EASIER AND MORE PLEASANT. WHEN BUYING TOOLS, SELECT ONES THAT ARE STURDY, RELIABLE AND COMFORTABLE TO USE. KEEP THEM CLOSE AT HAND FOR MAXIMUM CONVENIENCE.

Bead reamer

This can be used to expand or open plugged holes in beads and pearls.

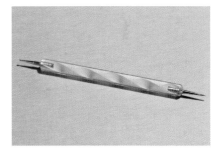

Camera

Take pictures of your work for posterity. They don't have to be professional-quality photos. Even simple photos taken with a standard camera provide you with an excellent record of your work.

Crochet hook

This is used to crochet wire to make intricate wire jewelry.

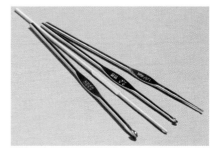

Idea notebook

Use this to jot down ideas you have for future projects.

Jeweler's hammer and block

Strike wire with a jeweler's hammer to harden it. The hammer head has a flat side and a round side. Use the flat side to flatten wire and the round to create a textured look. Always place the jewelry on the block before striking,

Large and small scissors

Scissors are used to cut thread, string, ribbon and fabric. Use delicate scissors for cutting close edges or trimming areas that are too narrow for other tools.

Magnifying glass

You may need this to make sure a jump ring is properly closed or to get a good look at particularly small pieces.

Mini files and sharpening stone

These are used to file wires. Use mini files for sharpening a wire tip finely to make a pin.

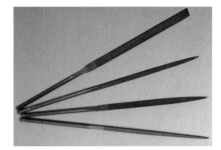

Needles

Keep various sizes on hand for the different objects you'll be stringing.

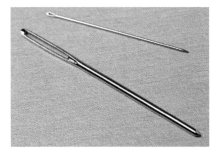

Pliers

I use chain-nose pliers (often two at the same time) for many projects. If you have only one pair, flat-nose or crimping pliers can substitute as a second.

Chain-nose pliers These are used for diverse purposes such as holding jump rings and jewelry parts, opening and closing jump rings, and flattening crimp beads and crimp ends. The inner edge of the arms is slightly textured, which prevents them from slipping and ensures a better grip. The tips of the pliers are pointed, allowing you to work in small areas.

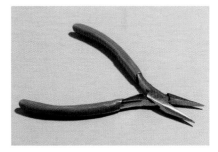

Crimping pliers These are specially designed for flattening crimp beads and crimp ends.

Flat-nose pliers These are used to bend wire, make spirals, and tuck in wire ends. They have arms that are flat and wide, making them useful for closing items such as large jump rings and metal chains with relatively thick links.

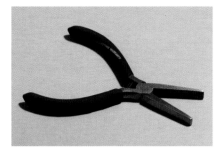

Round-nose pliers These are used to make, open, widen and close loops. They have rounded wide arms that narrow gradually towards the tips.

Ring mandrel

This cone-shaped rod is used to measure ring diameter. You can also use it to make wire loops of various sizes.

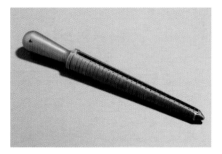

Sewing pins

These help secure objects to your work surface.

Stamps and stamp pad

These can be used to add images to fabric.

Tape measure and ruler

Use one that indicates both inches and centimeters.

Tweezers with magnifying glass

This is a helpful tool for picking up tiny beads and small jewel parts.

Wire cutters

There is a wide variety of cutting tools on the market, and many people have at least one or two types of cutters in their collection. I use the following wire cutters most often. For your own projects, choose the tool that feels most comfortable and best suits the type of wire you're using.

Flush cutters This sturdy tool is excellent for trimming head pins and eye pins and for cutting wire. It can also be used to trim beading wire and thread.

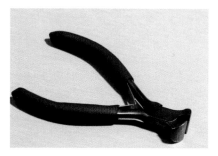

Side cutters This common tool is used to cut wire, especially in narrow places.

Wire nippers They are used to cut wire in narrow and delicate places.

Work surface

An appropriate work surface makes the jewelry-making process easier and more comfortable.

Cloth work surface Made from material that is soft and pleasant to the touch, this type of surface prevents materials from sliding. I suggest using skin-colored fabric that allows you to see how your jewelry will look when it is worn.

Work surface with measurements This type of surface features standard jewelry lengths and is excellent for making multistrand necklaces.

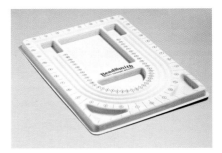

TECHNIQUES

BASIC JEWELRY-MAKING TECHNIQUES

Finishing ends with crimp beads

I usually use two crimp beads for finishing jewelry to ensure a secure finish.

1 String 2 crimp beads and 1 clasp (or split ring) onto the beading wire.

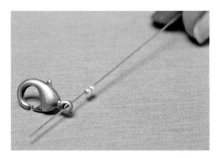

2 Make a loop at the end of the wire and insert the tip back into the crimp beads.

3 Flatten the crimp beads with chain-nose pliers. Trim excess wire with wire cutters.

Finishing ends with crimp beads and a bead tip

This simple technique creates a polished finish by concealing the crimp beads.

1 String 1 bead tip and 2 crimp beads onto the beading wire.

2 Flatten the crimp beads with the chain-nose pliers.

3 Trim the wire close to the flattened crimp beads.

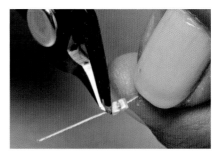

4 Draw the bead tip up to the flattened crimp beads and fold it over the beads to conceal them.

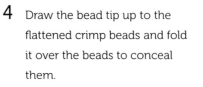

Securing ends with crimp ends

Crimp ends are generally strung onto chain or rope ends. They have three ribs and a loop at one end. The middle rib is flattened to secure.

1 String the crimp end onto the tip of the beading wire.

2 Using the chain-nose pliers, flatten the middle of the crimp end.

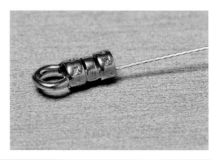

Securing ends with cord tips

Cord tips are generally strung onto cord and lace ends. They have three open sides and a loop at one end. The sides are folded over the cord, and each other, to secure.

1 Place the cord tip on the end of the cord.

2 Using the chain-nose pliers, fold the left side of the cord tip over the cord. Fold the right side of the cord tip over the left side. Press to secure.

Opening and closing jump rings

To open:

1 Hold a set of chain-nose pliers in each hand. Grasp each side of the jump ring with one set of pliers.

2 Move one set of pliers away from you and the other set of pliers towards you.

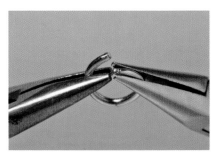

3 Move the pliers in opposite directions until the space between the ends of the jump ring is large enough for stringing.
Never open a jump ring by drawing the ends sideways away from each other.

To close:

1 Hold a set of pliers in each hand. Grasp each side of the open jump ring with one set of pliers.

2 Move the pliers that are farther from you towards you, and move the pliers that are closer to you away from you.

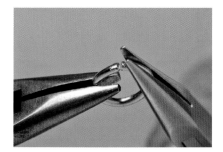

3 Move the pliers until the two ends of the jump ring meet.

4 If the jump ring doesn't close securely, hold it with your fingers or with 1 set of pliers. Using the other pliers, gently press one end of the jump ring inwards towards the middle of the jump ring. Turn the jump ring around and gently press the other end of the jump ring inwards until the ring is firmly closed.

Opening and closing chain links

This technique allows you to add components to unsoldered link chains. It also enables you use links from a chain as unusually sized jump rings. Note that this is different from opening and closing jump rings, which involves moving the sides in forward/backward directions.

To open:

1 Hold a set of pliers in each hand. Grasp each side of the link with one set of pliers.

2 Move the pliers away from each other in opposite, sideways directions.

To close:

1 Hold a set of pliers in each hand. Grasp each side of the open link with one set of pliers.

2 Bring the ends of the link together by bringing the pliers on each side of the link towards the original meeting point.

3 Press the sides of the link together with one set of pliers. Turn over the link and repeat on the other side.

Adding an extension chain

Attaching a short chain to one end of a necklace or bracelet makes the jewelry adjustable. It's a practical addition when making jewelry for a friend since you may not know the exact size.

1 Affix a lobster claw clasp onto one end of the necklace or bracelet.

2 Open a jump ring and string it through the last link at the other end of the jewelry. String on a short piece of chain, about 3" (7.5 cm) for necklaces and 1$^1/_2$" (4 cm) for bracelets, and close the jump ring.

WIRE TECHNIQUES

When working with wire, you can either work directly from the wire coil or cut pieces of wire from the coil and work with them according to a sketch or specific size. While the first method reduces the amount of wasted wire, I find it a bit less comfortable, so I tend to cut wire pieces in advance. To help save wire, I suggest making a sketch of the object you have in mind and practice making it with simple wire first to find out exactly how much you'll need. Another way of estimating the amount of wire you'll need is by practicing with a piece of cotton or wool string. Cut a piece of string and use it to trace your sketch. Measure the amount of string that was needed and add a bit extra for finishing. Use this as your estimate for the wire.

If the pieces of wire you trim in a project are long, save them for another project. If they are short, cut down on clutter by throwing them away.

Making a loop in a head pin or eye pin

When gathering materials for a specific project, make sure the head pins and eye pins you select are the right width and length.

1 String the bead or beads onto the head pin or eye pin.

2 Bend the head pin using chain-nose pliers or your fingers.

3 Trim the wire to ³/₈" (1 cm).

4 Grasp the tip of the wire with round-nose pliers and shape the wire into a loop.

5 Using chain-nose pliers, close the loop securely.

Connecting beaded eye pins

1 To connect two beaded pins, follow steps 1 to 4 (above) to make a loop, but don't close the loop.

2 Connect the open loop to the closed loop of another beaded pin; then close the loop securely.

Making a wrapped loop

Use this technique to hang beads and buttons neatly using wire or long pins.

1 String a bead, button or charm onto a piece of wire that is at least 2" (5 cm) longer than the bead.

2 Position the bead near the middle of the wire so that when the wires are bent and meet above the bead, one wire is about $^4/_5$" (2 cm) long and the other is $1^1/_5$" (3 cm) long.

3 Wrap the longer wire end around the shorter end 3 or 4 times to make a coil immediately above the bead.

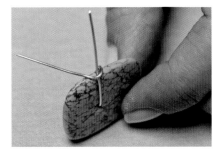
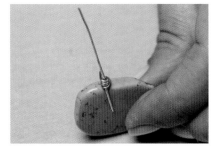

4 Shape the shorter end of wire into a loop. Close the loop.

Making loops for hanging top-drilled beads and drops

This technique allows you to hang items such as pendants, charms and beads.

1 String the bead/s or pendant/s onto a piece of wire and draw along to the middle of the wire.

2 Wrap together the two ends of wire several times above the bead/s. Shape the straight end of the wire into a loop.

Wrapping metal wire around readymade shapes

This technique allows you to integrate beads in diverse and interesting ways. Imagine a tiny dream catcher made with wire and beads.

1 Wrap the end of a piece of wire several times around a readymade shape to secure.

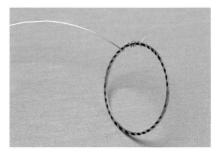

2 Draw the wire across the shape in any direction. Pull the wire as taut as possible using your fingers or pliers.

3 String on beads then wrap the wire around another point in the shape. Repeat steps 2 and 3 as desired.

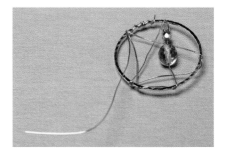

4 To finish, wrap the wire end several times around the shape and trim the tip. Press the tip against the shape using pliers.

Making coils

Wrap wire several times around a tubular object such as a ring mandrel or wooden rolling pin. This technique is often used to make rings or bracelets.

Making a tight spiral

1 Make a small, closed loop at one end of the wire using the round-nose pliers.

2 Grasp the loop with pliers that have flat, wide arms. (You may want to use pliers with silicone-coated jaws to avoid damaging the wire). Rotate the pliers in a clockwise direction while guiding the wire with your free hand so that the wire wraps tightly around the loop to form a spiral.

3 Continue rotating the spiral while holding the straight wire close to it.

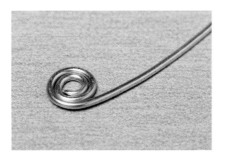

Once you master the basic spiral, vary its size and shape.

Making a loose spiral

1 The technique is similar to that of the tight spiral (above). This time, start with a small open loop at one end of the wire.

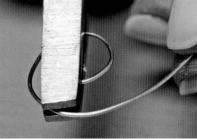

2 Use your fingers to maintain an even space between the rounds of wire as you wrap it into a spiral.

Practicing with a sketch and/or inexpensive wire

1 Draw a sketch of the item you want to make.

2 Place one end of a piece of inexpensive wire on the sketch and begin shaping the wire according to the outline of your sketch.

3 Once you've achieved the general shape, remove the wire from the sketch and continue shaping it using pliers and your fingers.

4 When you're satisfied with your model design, copy it using high-quality wire.

Striking wire with a hammer

Make wire harder and more stable and by striking it with a jeweler's hammer. Once wire has been hammered it is no longer flexible.

1 Place the wire shape on a block. For a flattened look, strike the object with the flat head of the hammer.

2 For a textured look, strike the object with the round head of the hammer.

TIPS

BUYING MATERIALS

• Enjoy the process of looking for materials and use your imagination.

• Shopping in jewelry supply stores can be hectic. The following strategies may help to make the experience more pleasant:

    * Bring an organized list of what you need to buy.

    * First find the items you need, then wander at leisure.

    * Ask a salesperson about new and innovative products.

    * If you buy something because it ignites your imagination, make a note of what you want to make with it.

• Planning a trip? Before you go, look online for information about stores, markets or fairs that may interest you. Some of the most interesting pieces of jewelry I make include elements that I found on my travels.

• Don't compromise on quality. It is possible to find excellent materials at reasonable prices.

• If you plan to buy in bulk, find a supplier who offers discounts for large purchases.

• Look for suppliers that constantly renew their supplies.

BEFORE YOU START

Start each project with a tidy workspace. It makes the creation process easier and much more pleasant.

From idea to creation

• Imagine your idea as though it is already finished, and being worn.

• Make a sketch of your idea, then make it with simple wire. When you're satisfied with the results, re-create it using more expensive wire.

• If you have many ideas but are short on time, sort the materials for each idea and place them in bag with a note or drawing.

• Store materials in an organized manner (by color, size or type) that works for you.

While you're working

- Have all the materials and tools you need for your project.
- Make sure all the materials are technically suited. For example, the wire is thin enough to string into the bead holes.
- Arrange the materials on a nonslip work surface.
- Measure the wire carefully—and leave enough room for attaching the clasp—before cutting it.
- Double check the length of all jewelry before affixing clasps. This is particularly important for bracelets, which you need to measure on your wrist (or someone else's) before finishing.

Finishing your project

- When your project is finished, put tools and leftover materials back in their places. It's relatively easy to clean up after a single project but considerably harder to tidy up a mess that has accumulated over several projects.
- Take a picture of the final piece. You'll have it as a souvenir if you plan on giving the jewelry away. Pictures also allow you to watch your own progress and development.
- Store finished pieces properly to help ensure their long life. For example, clothes hangers are great for hanging necklaces; a beautiful tray can be just right for storing bracelets.

Ready to start

Now that you have all the right tools and materials close at hand, you're ready to start. Make sure you have a comfortable work space and enough light. Relax, put on some music and enjoy. Remember that the process of making creative beaded jewelry is just as rewarding as wearing it!

Sleek Citrine Necklace

FINISHED MEASUREMENT

29^{1}/$_{2}$" (7 cm)

SKILL LEVEL

★ ☆ ☆ ☆ Easy

MATERIALS

2 silver-plated bead tips

4 silver-plated crimp beads

12" (30 cm) nylon-coated steel beading wire, 0.018" (0.45 mm) diameter

8 square citrine beads, about 1.5 cm

4 antique silver - (wire-wrapped) beads, 20 mm

2 antique silver - (wire-wrapped) beads, 16 mm

2 antique silver jump rings, 8 mm

2 antique silver thick links, 10 mm

24" (61 cm) dark silver-plated large-link chain

TOOLS

2 chain-nose pliers

Crimping pliers

Wire cutters

INSTRUCTIONS

1 String 1 bead tip and 2 crimp beads onto the beading wire.

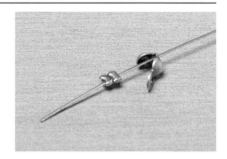

(CONTINUED ON PAGE 44)

(CONTINUED FROM PAGE 42)

2 Flatten the crimp beads, trim the excess wire and fold the bead tip over the crimp beads.

3 String beads onto the beading wire in the following order: 1 x citrine bead, 1 x 20 mm wire-wrapped bead, 1 x citrine bead, 1 x 16 mm wire-wrapped bead, 1 x citrine bead, 1 x 20 mm wire-wrapped bead, 1 x citrine bead, 1 x 16 mm wire-wrapped bead, 1 x citrine bead, 1 x 20 mm wire-wrapped bead, 2 x citrine beads, 1 x 20 mm wire-wrapped bead, 1 x citrine bead.

4 Repeat steps 1 and 2 to finish the necklace.

5 Open both 8 mm jump rings and string each one onto a bead tip. Close the jump rings.

6 Open both 10 mm links and string one onto each 8 mm jump ring. String one end of the silver chain through each 1 cm link and close the links. ◎

TIP THE LINKS USED TO CONNECT THE BEADED PART OF THE NECKLACE TO THE LARGE-LINK CHAIN WERE REMOVED FROM A MEDIUM-LINK CHAIN. IF YOU CAN'T FIND A CHAIN WITH UNSOLDERED LINKS, SIMPLY USE $^3/8$" (1 CM) JUMP RINGS INSTEAD.

Light Leafy Necklace

FINISHED MEASUREMENT
19" (48 cm)

SKILL LEVEL
★ ★ ☆ ☆ Intermediate

MATERIALS

78" (200 cm) silver-plated half-hard round wire, 32-gauge (0.2 mm), cut into two 39" (100 cm) pieces

78" (200 cm) bronze half-hard round wire, 32-gauge (0.2 mm), cut into two 39" (100 cm) pieces

39" (100 cm) gray half-hard round wire, 32-gauge (0.2 mm)

2 silver-plated cord tips

31 white or transparent glass leaf beads, top-drilled, front to back, in three sizes: 13 x 17 mm, 9 x 14 mm, 9 x 10 mm

2 jump rings, 6 mm

1 silver-plated split ring, 8 mm

1 silver-plated lobster claw clasp

TOOLS

Chain-nose or crimping pliers

Wire cutters

INSTRUCTIONS

1 Grasp all wires in one hand and string a cord tip onto the ends. Flatten the cord tip.

2 Move 2 wires aside and hold the other 3 wires together. String 1 leaf bead onto the wires and draw it down until it is about 2" (5 cm) from the cord tip.

3 Wrap the wires together above the leaf bead a few times to secure the leaf in place.

4 String another leaf bead onto the 3 wires and draw it down until it is about 2" (5 cm) from the first bead. Wrap the wire above the leaf a few times to secure the leaf.

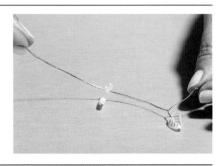

5 Repeat step 4 using various sizes of leaf beads until the necklace is the desired length. If you like, string 2 leaf beads at a time.

6 Hold together the 2 wires you moved aside in step 2 and string on a leaf bead. Draw it down the wires until it is between the first and second leaf beads that were strung on the first 3 wires. Wrap the wires on either side of the leaf bead to secure the leaf in place.

7 String another leaf bead onto the 2 wires and draw it down until it is between the second and third leaf bead on the first 3 wires. Wrap the wires on both sides of the leaf bead together to secure the leaf in place. Repeat this process until you reach the other end of the necklace.

8 Gather all 5 wire ends together and insert into a cord tip. Flatten the cord tip and trim excess wire.

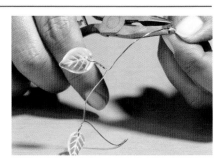

9 Open both jump rings and insert one into each cord tip. String the split ring onto one jump ring and the clasp onto the other jump ring. Close the jump rings. ◎

Linked Lava Rock Necklace

OPPOSITES ATTRACT IN THIS NECKLACE, WHICH FEATURES LARGE, ROUND LINKS AND LONG, DARK LAVA ROCKS. THE COMBINATION IS INTRIGUING AND STRIKING.

FINISHED MEASUREMENT

28¹/₂" (72 cm)

SKILL LEVEL

★ ☆ ☆ ☆　Easy

MATERIALS

7 finger-shaped lava rock beads, top-drilled, side-to-side, 30-50 mm x 10-15 mm

7 silver-plated eye pins, 1¹/₂" (4 cm)

6 silver-plated jump rings, 6 mm

24" (61 cm) silver-plated unsoldered link chain

TOOLS

Round-nose pliers

Wire cutters

INSTRUCTIONS

1 String a lava rock bead onto an eye pin. Trim the eye pin to ³/₈" (1 cm) and make a closed loop.

(CONTINUED ON PAGE 50)

(CONTINUED FROM PAGE 48)

2 Repeat step 1 to string all the lava rock beads onto eye pins.

3 Arrange the beads in a row on your work surface. Play with the order until you are satisfied with their combination.

4 Open a jump ring and string it through adjacent loops in adjacent beads. Close the jump ring.

5 Repeat step 4 until all the beads are connected.

6 Open the links at both ends of the chain. Insert these links onto the loops on both sides of the beads and close the links. ☺

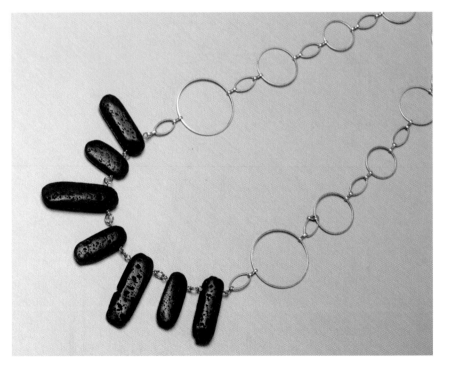

Creative Wire Jewelry

Graciously Gold Pearl Cluster Necklace

DRESS UP A PLAIN LINK CHAIN WITH SOME PRETTY PEARL CLUSTERS. FOR EASY-TO-MAKE MATCHING EARRINGS, SEE PAGE 118.

FINISHED MEASUREMENT

31$^{1}/_{2}$" (80 cm)

SKILL LEVEL

★ ☆ ☆ ☆ Easy

MATERIALS

3 white freshwater pearl cluster beads, 10 mm

3 gold-plated eye pins, 1$^{1}/_{4}$" (3 cm)

8 oval gold-plated jump rings, 6 mm

30" (76 cm) gold-plated large-link chain, divided into 4 pieces: 1 x 2" (5 cm), 1 x 7" (18 cm), 1 x 4" (10 cm), 1 x 17" (43 cm)

1 gold-plated toggle clasp

TOOLS

Wire cutters

Round-nose pliers

INSTRUCTIONS

1   String each pearl cluster onto an eye pin. Trim each eye pin to $^{3}/_{8}$" (1 cm) and make a closed loop.

2 Open 6 jump rings and use them to connect the bead clusters and chain pieces in the following order: one 2" (5 cm) chain, one pearl cluster, one 17" (43 cm) chain, one pearl cluster, one 4" (10 cm) chain, one pearl cluster, one 7" (18 cm) chain. Close the jump rings.

3 Open 2 jump rings and string one onto each end of the necklace. String half the clasp onto each jump ring and close the jump rings. ◎

Gold Nugget Leather Necklace

THIS VERSATILE DESIGN CAN BE WORN LONG OR SHORT. IT'S EASY TO MAKE BUT PACKED WITH PRESENCE AND CAN BE WORN DAY OR NIGHT.

FINISHED MEASUREMENT

33" (84 cm)

SKILL LEVEL

★ ☆ ☆ ☆   Easy

MATERIALS

12" (30 cm) dark brown leather lace

2 gold-plated cord tips

2 gold-plated jump rings, 6 mm

20" (51 cm) gold-plated large-link chain

1 gold-plated lobster claw clasp

TOOLS

2 chain-nose pliers

INSTRUCTIONS

1   Insert each end of the leather lace into a cord tip. Flatten the cord tips.

2   Open a jump ring and string it through one cord tip and the link at one end of the chain. Close the jump ring.

3   Open a jump ring and string it through the other cord tip and the clasp. Close jump ring. ◎

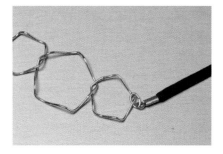

Tranquilly Turquoise Necklace

THIS LONG CHAIN OF SMOOTH CERAMIC BEADS AND SILVER HIGHLIGHTS EVOKES A LOVELY SENSE OF CALM.

FINISHED MEASUREMENT

38" (96.5 cm)

SKILL LEVEL

★ ★ ☆ ☆ Intermediate

MATERIALS

33 diamond turquoise ceramic beads, 13 x 15 mm

33 silver-plated eye pins, 1¹/₄" (3 cm)

1 square turquoise ceramic bead, 10 x 10 mm

2 round turquoise ceramic beads, 13 mm

1 silver-plated eye pin, 2³/₄" (7 cm)

1 silver-plated hoop, 35 mm

1 silver-plated heart, 30 mm

5 silver-plated jump rings, 6 mm

6 silver-plated jump rings, 4 mm

59" (150 cm) thin silver-plated small-link chain

TOOLS

Round-nose pliers

Wire cutters

INSTRUCTIONS

1 String a diamond turquoise bead onto a 1¹/₄" (3 cm) eye pin. Trim the eye pin to ³/₈" (1 cm) and make a loop but don't close it.

Creative Wire Jewelry

(CONTINUED ON PAGE 58)

(CONTINUED FROM PAGE 56)

2 Repeat step 1 to string 32 diamond beads onto eye pins.

3 Connect the decorated eye pins in a chain by stringing the open loop at one end of each eye pin into the closed loop of another eye pin. Close the loops.

4 String 1 diamond turquoise bead, 1 square turquoise bead and 1 round turquoise bead onto a 2³/₄" (7 cm) eye pin. Trim the eye pin to ³/₈" (1 cm) and make a loop but don't close it.

5 String 1 round turquoise bead onto a 1¹/₄" (3 cm) eye pin. Trim the eye pin to ³/₈" (1 cm) and make a loop but don't close it.

6 String the loop through one end of the diamond bead chain you made in step 3 and close the loop.

7 Open two 4 mm jump rings. String one end of the silver-plated chain onto one jump ring. Measure 4" (10 cm) along the chain; then string on the other jump ring.

8 Fold the chain, bring it back to the first jump ring, and string it onto the jump ring. Fold the chain, bring it back to the second jump ring, and string it onto the jump ring.

9 Repeat step 7 until the chain has been strung 10 times between the 2 jump rings. Close the jump rings.

10 Open a jump ring and use it to connect the free end of the round bead and the group of chains strung in steps 7 to 9. Close the jump ring.

11 Open a jump ring and use it to connect the other end of the group of chains and the 35 mm hoop. Close the jump ring.

12 Open a jump ring and use it to connect the 35 mm hoop and the eye pin with the diamond, square and round beads. Close the jump ring.

13 Open a jump ring and use it to connect the other end of the eye pin with the diamond, square and round bead to the heart. Close the jump ring. ◎

Turquoise Cairn Necklace

CAIRNS ARE SMALL ROCK PILES ERECTED AS COMMEMORATIVE MONUMENTS OR WILDERNESS TRAIL MARKERS. IN THIS DESIGN, THE CAIRN IS CONSTRUCTED USING DARK-VEINED TURQUOISE BEADS.

FINISHED MEASUREMENT

Necklace: 33" (84 cm)

Pendant: 5" (13 cm)

SKILL LEVEL

★ ★ ☆ ☆ Intermediate

MATERIALS

2 silver-plated jump rings, 5 mm

40" (101 cm) silver-plated, large-link chain, cut into 6 pieces: 1 x 30" (76 cm), 1 x 2³/₄" (7 cm), 1 x 2¹/₂" (6.4 cm), 1 x 2¹/₄"(5.7 cm), 1 x 2" (5 cm), 1 x 1¹/₂" (4 cm)

1 silver-plated eye pin, 2³/₄" (7 cm)

7 flat turquoise beads, middle-drilled, front-to-back, 30–40 mm

TOOLS

Wire cutters

Flat-nose pliers

Round-nose pliers

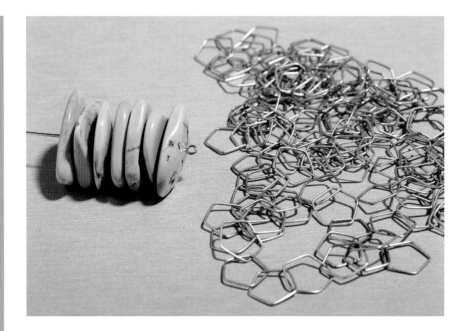

INSTRUCTIONS

1   Open a jump ring and string it through the loop in the eye pin. String on the 5 short chains; then close the jump ring.

2 String 7 turquoise beads onto the eye pin, in any order you like. Trim the eye pin to $^3/_8$" (1 cm) and make a closed loop.

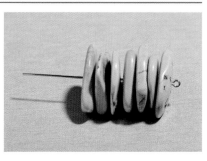

3 Open the remaining jump ring. String it through the loop at the top of the eye pin and the links on both ends of the 30" (76 cm) chain. Close the jump ring. ◎

TIP THIS VERY SIMPLE TECHNIQUE ALLOWS YOU TO CREATE A VARIETY OF NECKLACES WITH EASE. YOU CAN VARY THE NECKLACES BY USING DIFFERENT TYPES OF CHAINS, CHAIN LENGTHS, AND BEADS OR STONES. USING THE SAME TECHNIQUE, YOU CAN PRODUCE VERY DIFFERENT RESULTS.

Golden Bouquet Necklace

THIS PRETTY NECKLACE IS PERFECT FOR
WEARING TO A SUNNY SUNDAY BRUNCH.
I SUGGEST THAT YOU FIRST PRACTICE MAKING
FLOWERS WITH INEXPENSIVE METAL WIRE.
TO COMPLEMENT THIS NECKLACE, MAKE
THE DANGLING FLOWER EARRINGS
(PAGES 120 TO 122).

FINISHED MEASUREMENT

47¼" (120 cm)

SKILL LEVEL

★ ★ ★ ★ Challenging

MATERIALS

82" (208 cm) gold-plated or gold-filled half-hard round wire, 20-gauge (0.8 mm), cut into 5 pieces: 3 x 20" (51 cm) and 2 x 10" (40 cm)

56" (142 cm) gold-plated small link chain, cut into 3 pieces: 1 x 22" (56 cm), 1 x 18" (46 cm), 1 x 16" (41 cm)

4 gold-plated jump rings, 6 mm

TOOLS

Round-nose pliers

Wire cutters

INSTRUCTIONS

1 Prepare the flowers: Gently bend 1 piece of wire near the middle, using pliers or your hands, to make 2 rounded petals. Continue bending the wire to make 5 rounded petal shapes.

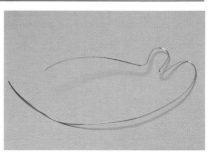

Creative Wire Jewelry

(CONTINUED ON PAGE 64)

(CONTINUED FROM PAGE 62)

2 Bring the wire ends together and wrap one end a few times around the other end, leaving a small tail. This tail will be used to connect the flowers to each other.

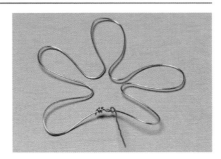

3 Repeat steps 1 and 2 to make 3 large flowers and 2 small flowers.

4 Place the 3 large flowers in a row with all the tails oriented in the same direction.

5 String the tail of the rightmost flower into the adjacent petal in the middle flower; wrap it a few times around the wire to secure. Trim the tail end and tuck in the tip.

6 Draw the tail of the middle flower between 2 petals in the adjacent flower; wrap the tail around the wire a few times to secure. Trim the end.

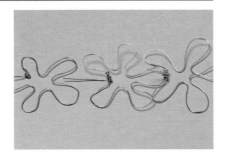

7 Place the 2 small flowers in a row with tails oriented in the same direction. Repeat step 5 to connect the first flower to the second flower. Wrap the tail of the second flower to itself, to create a similar wire wrap.

8 To assemble the necklace: open a jump ring and draw it through the end link of the 22" (56 cm) chain and the flower at one end of the 3-flower chain. Close the jump ring.

9 Open a jump ring and draw it through the other end of this chain and through one of the flowers in the 2-flower chain. Close the jump ring.

10 Open a jump ring and draw it through one end of the 18" (46 cm) and 16" (41 cm) chains. Draw the jump ring through the free end of the 3-flower chain and close the jump ring.

11 Open a jump ring and draw it through the other end of the 18" (46 cm) and 16" (41 cm) chains. Draw the jump ring through the free end of the 2-flower chain and close the jump ring. ©

Wavy Wire and Leather Lace Necklace

THIS VERY LONG NECKLACE CAN BE WORN IN DIFFERENT WAYS: KEEP IT LONG, TIE THE LACE TO MAKE IT A BIT SHORTER, OR WRAP IT TWICE AROUND YOUR NECK.

FINISHED MEASUREMENT
75" (190 cm)

SKILL LEVEL
★ ★ ★ ★ Challenging

MATERIALS

32" (81 cm) silver-plated half-hard round wire, 20-gauge (0.8 mm), cut into two 16" (40 cm) pieces

40" (101 cm) brown suede lace, 1 cm wide, cut into two 20" (50 cm) pieces

Three 32" (82 cm) silver-plated thin chains, with cord tips and loops at both ends

2 silver-plated jump rings, 5 mm

TOOLS

Round-nose pliers

Chain-nose pliers

Scissors

INSTRUCTIONS

1   Make a small closed loop at one end of one piece of wire. Bend the wire about 1" (2.5 cm) from the loop to make a U shape.

2   Continue bending the wire to make a series of U shapes along the entire length of the wire. Make a loop at the other end of the wire but don't close the loop.

(CONTINUED ON PAGE 68)

(CONTINUED FROM PAGE 66)

3 Repeat steps 1 and 2 with the other piece of wire.

4 String one end of all 3 chains onto one of the wavy wires via the open loop at the bottom of the wires. Draw the first and second chain up the wire and position them on different U-shaped loops. Leave the third chain inside the loop at the bottom of the wire and close the loop.

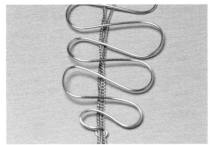

5 String the other end of all 3 chains onto the other wavy wire and position each chain in the corresponding place on this wire. Close the loop at the bottom of the wire.

6 Open one jump ring and string through the top loop of one wavy wire. Close the jump ring. String the end of one leather lace through the jump ring, allow for a 1" (2.5 cm) tail, and tie a secure knot.

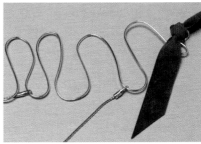

7 Repeat step 6 with the other wavy wire and the other piece of leather. Cut both ends of each lace on an angle. ◎

Marvelous Mesh Necklace

I ONLY RECENTLY BEGAN INTEGRATING PLASTIC MESH INTO MY WORK AND I'M DELIGHTED WITH THE RESULTS. MESH IS EASY TO WORK WITH AND IT PRODUCES UNEXPECTED AND INTERESTING RESULTS.

FINISHED MEASUREMENT

22" (56 cm)

SKILL LEVEL

★ ★ ★ ★ Challenging

MATERIALS

24" (61 cm) nylon-coated steel beading wire, 0.018" (0.45 mm) diameter

20" (51 cm) black plastic mesh tube, 16 mm diameter

2 silver-plated cord tips

34 round silver-plated beads, 8 mm

32" (80 cm) pieces of silver-plated half-hard round wire, 20-gauge (0.8 mm), cut into eight 4" (10 cm) pieces

7 round silver-plated beads, 14 mm

2 silver-plated jump rings, 6 mm

1 silver-plated split ring, 8 mm

1 silver-plated lobster claw clasp

TOOLS

Flat-nose pliers

Round-nose pliers

Wire cutters

INSTRUCTIONS

1 Insert the beading wire into the plastic mesh tube. Line up the end of the wire with the end of the tube and insert these ends into a cord tip. Flatten the cord tip. The beading wire will extend about 4" (10 cm) beyond the other end of the mesh tube.

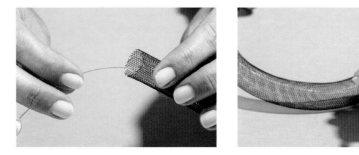

2 String seventeen 8 mm beads onto the beading wire, inserting them into the plastic mesh tube. Draw the beads along the wire until they reach the cord tip.

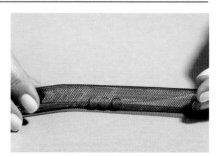

3 Wrap 1 piece of wire about 10 times around the mesh tube immediately above the beads, securing the beads in place.

4 String one 14 mm bead onto the beading wire (and inside the tube) and draw it along the wire until it is adjacent to the wrapped wire.

5 Wrap 1 piece of wire about 10 times around the mesh tube immediately above the bead, securing the bead in place.

6 Repeat steps 4 and 5 to string the rest of the 14 mm beads onto the wire. String seventeen 8 mm beads onto the beading wire. Trim the end of the beading wire and wire mesh so that they are even; then insert these ends into a cord tip. Flatten the cord tip.

7 Open both jump rings and string one onto each cord tip. String the clasp onto one jump ring and the split ring onto the other jump ring. Close the jump rings. ◎

Inspired Autumn Choker

Leaves are traditionally a sign of new beginnings; this design is no exception. The necklace features a combination of stamped fabric, wire and chain. It requires more than a few steps to make, so enjoy the process.

FINISHED MEASUREMENT

Choker: 12½" (32 cm)

Pendant: 2¾" (7 cm)

SKILL LEVEL

★ ★ ★ ★ Challenging

MATERIALS

Leaf-shaped stamp, 3½ x 1" (9 x 2.5 cm)

Light brown fabric dye

1 piece coarse, cream-colored cotton fabric, 8" x 8" (20 x 20 cm)

Sketching materials and/or inexpensive metal wire

2 silver-plated cord tips

3 silver-plated jump rings, 5 mm

48" (122 cm) silver-plated half-hard round wire, 18-gauge (1 mm), cut into 4 pieces: 3 x 12" (30 cm) and 1 x 14" (36 cm)

40" (101 cm) silver-plated thin-link chain

1 silver-plated split ring, 8 mm

1 silver-plated lobster claw clasp

TOOLS

2 chain-nose pliers

Round-nose pliers

Wire cutters

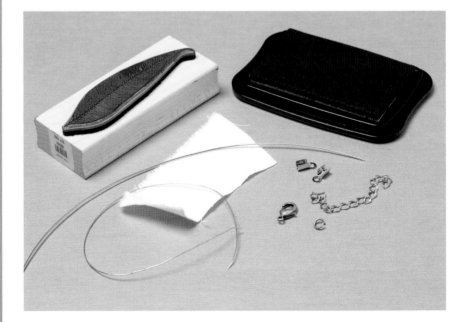

(CONTINUED ON PAGE 74)

(CONTINUED FROM PAGE 72)

INSTRUCTIONS

1 Stamp 2 leaf shapes onto the fabric and set aside to dry. When the ink is dry, cut out the leaves, leaving a $1/8$" (3 mm) margin all around the leaf and a 15 x 5 mm margin along the top.

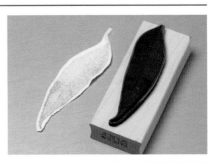

2 Tuck the fabric above the leaf into a cord tip and flatten the cord tip to secure. String a jump ring onto each cord tip and close the jump rings.

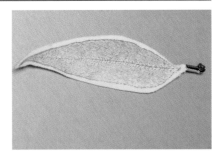

3 Draw a sketch of 3 leaves and/or practice shaping the leaves with inexpensive wire. Make the wire leaves slightly larger than the stamped leaves and include a small loop at the top of each leaf. When you are satisfied with the sketches, copy them with the 12" (30 cm) pieces of wire.

4 Make a loop at one end of the 14" (36 cm) piece of wire and shape the rest of the wire into a ring that fits comfortably around the neck.

5 String 1 wire leaf and 1 fabric leaf onto the choker.

6 String the first link of the chain onto the choker. Continue stringing links onto the choker, one after another, until you have filled about 2" (5 cm) of the choker with links. String on 1 wire leaf.

7 Continue stringing the chain onto the choker until you have filled another 2" (5 cm) of the choker with links. Ensure the length of chain on either side of the wire leaf is even. Cut the chain and save the excess for step 9.

8 String 1 wire leaf and 1 fabric leaf onto the choker.

9 Make a closed loop at the other end of the choker. Open 2 jump rings and string one on each loop at each end of the choker. Cut the excess chain you trimmed in step 7 in half and string each half onto one of the jump rings. Close the jump rings.

10 Open 2 jump rings and string them through the free end of each piece of chain. String the split ring onto a jump ring and close the jump ring. String the clasp onto the other jump ring and close the jump ring. ◎

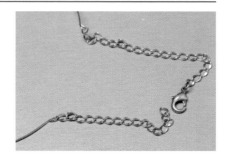

TIP THIS NECKLACE FEATURES AN EXTENSION CHAIN THAT ALLOWS YOU TO LENGTHEN THE NECKLACE A BIT. THIS SIMPLE TECHNIQUE CAN BE USED TO ADD LENGTH TO ALMOST ANY NECKLACE.

Linked Loops and Squares Necklace

THE GEMSTONES IN THIS VERSATILE NECKLACE ARE RICH AND BEAUTIFUL. FOR A RUSTIC LOOK, WEAR IT WITH A PAIR OF JEANS; IF YOU'RE DRESSING UP FOR A NIGHT OUT, PAIR IT WITH A SIMPLE BLACK DRESS.

FINISHED MEASUREMENT

34¼" (87 cm)

SKILL LEVEL

★ ★ ★ ☆ Advanced

MATERIALS

11 yd (10 m) silver-plated half-hard round wire, 24-gauge (0.5 mm)

1 asymetrical pewter hoop, 45 mm

3 rectangular carnelian beads, top-to-bottom, middle-drilled, 32 x 27 x 5 mm

3 silver-plated eye pins, 2" (5 cm)

19 silver-plated jump rings, 6 mm

TOOLS

2 chain-nose pliers

Round-nose pliers

Wire cutters

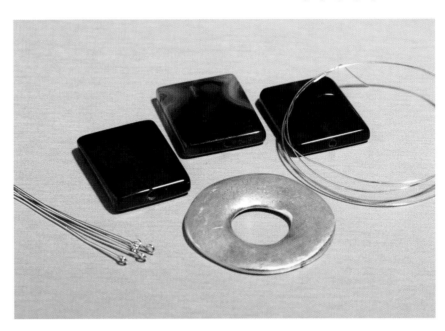

TIP TO MAKE THE LINKS IN THIS CHAIN, WRAP THE WIRE AROUND YOUR FINGERS. ADJUST THE SIZE OF THE LINKS TO YOUR OWN PREFERENCE.

(CONTINUED ON PAGE 78)

(CONTINUED FROM PAGE 77)

INSTRUCTIONS

1 Cut a 20" (51 cm) piece of wire. Grasp one end of the wire with your thumb and index finger and wrap it around three fingers to make a loop. You can vary the loop size, as desired, by positioning your fingers differently.

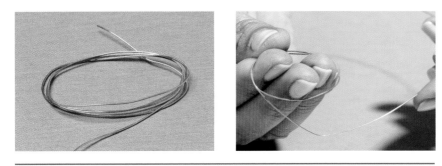

2 When you're happy with the size and shape of the loop, wrap the wire 3 more times around your fingers to make a 4-strand loop. Twist the end of the wire a few times around the 4-strand loop to secure. Trim the wire.

3 Repeat steps 1 and 2 another 15 times to make a total of 16 wire loops that are similar in size and shape.

4 Cut a 1¹/₂ yd (1.5 m) piece of wire and wrap it around the pewter hoop, from the middle of the hoop to the outside. Continue wrapping the hoop until it is completely covered with wire—about 80 wraps. Tuck the end of the wire under the wrapped wires at the back of the hoop to secure. Trim the wire.

5 Cut an 11" (28 cm) piece of wire. Insert one end of the wire into the middle of the wrapped pewter hoop and draw it through one of the loops you made in step 3. Wrap the wire to make a 4-strand loop connecting the pewter hoop to the wire loop. Secure the new loop by wrapping the free end of wire a few times.

6 Cut another 11" (28 cm) piece of wire and wrap it around the other side of the wrapped pewter hoop. Wrap it into a 4-strand loop that is similar in size to the one you made in step 5 and secure the loop by wrapping the free end of wire a few times.

7 String each carnelian bead onto an eye pin. Trim each eye pin to ³/₈" (1 cm) and make a closed loop.

8 Open the jump rings and use them to connect the necklace in the following order: 1 carnelian bead, 8 handmade loops, 1 carnelian bead, 3 handmade wire loops, 1 carnelian bead, 5 handmade wire loops. Connect the last wire loop to the

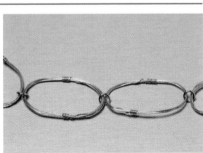 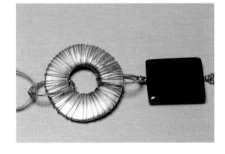

free loop on the wrapped pewter hoop. Connect the other loop on the hoop to the first carnelian bead. You can open the loop on the bead to do this, or use a jump ring. Close the jump rings. ©

Charming Chain and Agate Necklace

THIS LONG NECKLACE IS AN EXCELLENT EXAMPLE OF JEWELRY THAT MAKES AN OUTFIT. WEAR IT WITH A SIMPLE BLACK, WHITE OR GRAY DRESS TO MAXIMIZE ITS IMPACT. FOR JUST THE RIGHT EFFECT, POSITION THE 10 MM RING AT THE NAPE OF YOUR NECK WHEN YOU WEAR IT.

FINISHED MEASUREMENT

41³/₄" (106 cm)

SKILL LEVEL

★ ★ ★ ☆ Advanced

MATERIALS

12¹/₂ yd (11.5 m) silver-plated small-link chain

30 delicate jump rings, 3 mm

12 jump rings, 6 mm

4 round polished agate beads, 16 mm

4 silver-plated eye pins, 1¹/₄" (3 cm)

1 silver-plated hoop, 3.5 cm

1 silver-plated heart, 3 cm

1 silver-plated soldered link, 10 mm

TOOLS

Flat-nose pliers

Round-nose pliers

Wire cutters

INSTRUCTIONS

1   Prepare the chain clusters: Cut the chain into 75 pieces, each measuring 6" (15 cm) long.

2   Divide the chain pieces into 5 groups, so that each group has 15 chains.

(CONTINUED ON PAGE 82)

(CONTINUED FROM PAGE 80)

3 Open one 3 mm jump ring and string on the end link of 5 chain pieces. Close the jump ring.

4 Open another 3 mm jump ring and string it through the other end link of these 5 chains. Close the jump ring.

5 Repeat steps 3 and 4 another 2 times to form 3 small chain clusters with the 15 chains in one group.

6 Open a 6 mm jump ring and string it through the 3 mm jump rings at one end of these 3 small chain clusters. Close the jump ring.

7 Open another 6 mm jump ring and string it through the 3 mm jump rings at the other end of these 3 small chain clusters. Close the jump ring. You'll now have one large chain cluster.

8 Repeat steps 3 to 7 another 4 times to make a total of five large chain clusters.

9 String each agate bead onto an eye pin. Trim each eye pin to ³/₈" (1 cm) and make a closed loop.

10 Open the remaining 6 mm jump rings and use them to connect the necklace components in the following order: 1 chain cluster; 3 agate beads; 1 chain cluster; 1 hoop; 1 chain cluster; 1 agate bead; 1 chain cluster; 1 heart; 1 chain cluster.

11 Open the jump rings on both sides of the necklace, string them through the 10 mm soldered link, and close the jump rings. ◎

TIP MAKE SURE THAT THE 3 MM JUMP RINGS ARE THIN ENOUGH FOR STRINGING THROUGH THE LINKS IN THE CHAIN.

Sanctuary at Sea Necklace

Longing for a barefoot stroll along the beach? This necklace evokes the wonders of the sea with its starfish, conch and pearly seashell.

FINISHED MEASUREMENT
40" (102 cm)

SKILL LEVEL
★ ★ ★ ★   Challenging

MATERIALS

Starfish
Sketching materials and/or inexpensive wire

8" (20 cm) sterling silver half-hard round wire, 16-gauge (1.3 mm)

1½" (4 cm) sterling silver half-hard round wire, 24-gauge (0.5 mm)

Shell
Sketching materials and/or inexpensive wire

8" (20 cm) sterling silver half-hard round wire, 16-gauge (1.3 mm)

17" (35 cm) sterling silver half-hard round wire, 24-gauge (0.5 mm), cut into 2 pieces: 1 x 2" (5 cm) and 1 x 12" (30 cm)

40 white potato pearls, 4–5 mm

Snail
Sketching materials and/or inexpensive wire

10" (25 cm) sterling silver half-hard round wire, 16-gauge (1.3 mm)

Necklace
6 silver-plated jump rings, 5 mm

34" (86 cm) silver-plated small-link chain

TOOLS

Round-nose pliers

Chain-nose pliers

Wire cutters

Jeweler's hammer and block

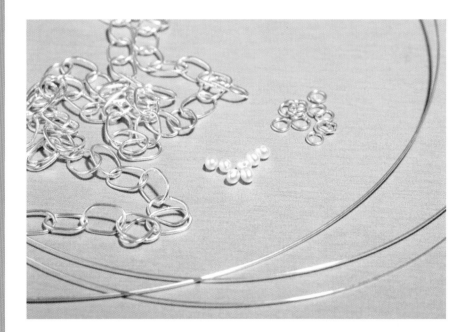

INSTRUCTIONS

Starfish

1 Draw a sketch of a star and/or practice making one with inexpensive wire. Shape the 16-gauge (1.3 mm) wire into a star shape using your fingers and pliers.

2 Hold the wire ends together and wrap with the thinner wire.

3 Place the star on the block and strike it with the round side of the hammer head. Make sure you don't hit the star in the area where the thinner wire is wrapped.

Shell

4 Draw a sketch of a shell and/or practice making one with inexpensive wire. Shape the 16-gauge (1.3 mm) wire into a shell shape.

5 Hold the wire ends together and wrap together with the 2" (5 cm) piece of 24-gauge (0.5 mm) wire.

6 Place the shell on the block and strike it with the round side of the hammer head. Make sure you don't hit the shell in the area where the thinner wire is wrapped.

7 Wrap the tip of the 12" (30 cm) piece of 24-gauge (0.5 mm) wire around the base of the shell a few times to secure.

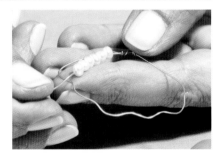

8 String on 7 or 8 pearls (enough to fill the space up to the top of the shell) and bring the wire to the top of the shell. Wrap the wire a few times around the top of the shell until it is between the second and third wave.

(CONTINUED ON PAGE 86)

Creative Wire Jewelry

(CONTINUED FROM PAGE 84)

9 String on 8 or 9 pearls (enough to fill the space down to the base of the shell) then wrap the wire twice around the base of the shell.

10 String on 8 or 9 pearls and bring the wire to the top of the shell, between the third and fourth wave. Wrap it around the top of the shell until it is between the fourth and fifth wave, then string on 8 or 9 beads. Continue with this process until pearls have been strung up and down the shell at regular intervals.

Snail

11 Draw a sketch of a snail and/or practice making one with inexpensive wire. Work the wire into a snail shape using your fingers and the pliers. Secure the shape by wrapping one end of the wire.

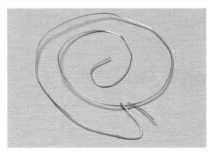

12 Place the snail on the block and strike it with the round side of the hammer head. Make sure you don't hit the snail in the area where the thinner wire is wrapped.

Connecting the pieces

13 Open the jump rings. String a jump ring through the top of the snail and one end of the chain. Close the jump ring.

14 String a jump ring through the bottom of the snail and the top of the shell. Close the jump ring.

15 String 3 jump rings through the bottom of the shell, at even intervals, and through the top of the star. Close the jump rings.

16 String a jump ring through the bottom of the star and the free end of the chain. Close the jump ring. ©

TIP You can use this technique to make any shape you like. Just think of a theme and create a shape to match. You can also connect the shapes using chains of various lengths.

Treasures of the Sea Bracelet

Every shell is distinct, which guarantees that your version of this bracelet will be unique. Another distinct feature of this bracelet is its handmade clasp.

FINISHED MEASUREMENT

8¼" (21 cm)

SKILL LEVEL

★ ★ ☆ ☆ Intermediate

MATERIALS

40" (101 cm) gold-plated half-hard round wire, 24-gauge (0.5 mm), cut into two 20" (50.5 cm) pieces

22 round shells, middle-drilled, 23 mm

6 round shells, middle-drilled, 18 mm

10 round shells, middle-drilled, 14 mm

TOOLS

Wire cutters

INSTRUCTIONS

1 Hold both wire pieces together and string on two 23 mm shells. Orient the shells so that the dull sides are touching.

TIP When stringing the shells, make sure the shiny side always faces upwards.

2 Draw the shells to the middle of the wires and wrap the wires together a few times above the shells.

3 Separate the wires into pairs. String a 23 mm and 18 mm shell onto one pair of wires and twist the wires together to secure. String two 23 mm shells and an 18 mm shell onto the other pair of wires and twist together to secure. Twist all 4 wires together a few times.

4 Repeat step 3 several more times, stringing 2 to 5 shells onto each pair of wires every time, alternating the sizes of the shells you select, until the bracelet is the desired length.

5 Wrap the two pairs of wires together a few times. Shape the wires into a loop that is large enough to fit over the two shells you secured in step 2.

6 Wrap the ends of the wires several times around the base of the loop and press in the tips of the wire. ©

Springtime Garden Bracelet

FINISHED MEASUREMENT

8½" (22 cm)

SKILL LEVEL

★ ★ ☆ ☆ Intermediate

MATERIALS

12" (30 cm) gold-plated half-hard round wire, 16-gauge (1.3 mm), cut into six 2" (5 cm) pieces

6 white glass leaf beads, 18 x 12 mm

6 green glass leaf beads, 16 x 10 mm

5 light pink disk glass beads, middle-drilled, top-to-bottom, 28 mm

5 gold-plated eye pins, 2" (5 cm)

1 gold-plated leaf-shaped toggle clasp

7 gold-plated jump rings, 6 mm

TOOLS

Chain-nose

Round-nose pliers

Wire cutters

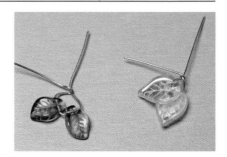

INSTRUCTIONS

1   String 2 white leaf beads onto a piece of gold wire. Bring the beads to the middle of the wire and wrap the wires together above the beads. Twist one several times around the other wire then trim the straight wire to ³/₈" (1 cm) and make a loop.

Creative Wire Jewelry

90

(CONTINUED ON PAGE 92)

(CONTINUED FROM PAGE 90)

2 Repeat step 1 with pairs of white and green leaf beads to make 6 sets of hanging leaves.

3 String each light pink bead onto an eye pin. Trim each eye pin to $^{3}/_{8}$" (1 cm) and make a closed loop.

4 Open a jump ring and string it through the loop on a light pink bead. String on a pair of leaf beads and another light pink bead. Close the jump ring.

5 Repeat step 4 to connect the rest of the light pink beads, alternating between green and white pairs of leaf beads.

6 Open 2 jump rings and string one through the loop at each end of the bracelet. String half the clasp and 1 pair of leaf beads onto each jump ring and close the jump rings. ©

Sparkling Silver Spiral Bracelet

THIS BEAUTIFUL BRACELET COMBINES STRIPED RECTANGULAR ROCKS WITH SHINY METAL SPIRALS. I SUGGEST MAKING A FEW SPIRALS WITH INEXPENSIVE WIRE BEFORE MOVING ONTO THE STERLING SILVER WIRE.

FINISHED MEASUREMENT

8½" (22 cm)

SKILL LEVEL

★ ☆ ☆ ☆ Easy

MATERIALS

6 flat rectangular agate beads, 20 x 15 x 5 mm

6 sterling silver eye pin, 2" (5 cm)

14" (35 cm) sterling silver half-hard round wire, 18-gauge (1 mm), cut into seven 2" (5 cm) pieces

1 sterling silver toggle clasp

7 sterling silver jump rings, 6 mm

TOOLS

Round-nose pliers

Wire cutters

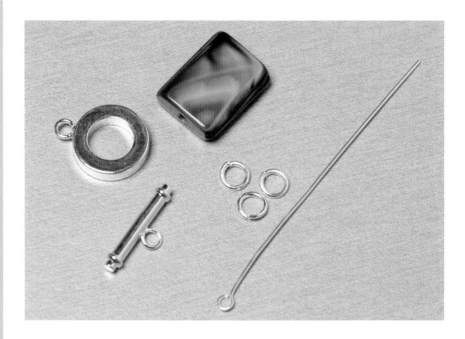

INSTRUCTIONS

1   String each agate bead onto an eye pin. Trim each eye pin to $^3/_8$" (1 cm) and make a closed loop.

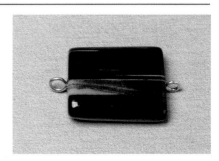

Bracelets

93

2 Twist 1 piece of wire into a spiral shape with a $^3/_8$" (1 cm) straight end. Shape the straight end into a loop.

3 Repeat step 2 with the other 6 pieces of wire.

4 Open a jump ring and string it through the loop on half the clasp and the loop at one end of an agate bead.

5 String on a wire spiral and close the jump ring.

6 Open a jump ring and string it through the loop at the other end of the agate bead. String the jump ring through one spiral, then through the loop in another agate bead. Close the jump ring.

7 Repeat step 6 to connect all the agate beads and spirals.

8 Open a jump ring and string it through the free loop on the last agate bead. String on a silver spiral and the other half of the clasp. Close the jump ring. ◎

To make matching Sparkling Spiral Earrings (pictured here) see page 119.

Totally Twisted Bracelet

This bracelet is a fantastic complement to the Sleek Citrine Necklace (pages 42 to 44). Replace the citrine with a different gemstone for a variation.

FINISHED MEASUREMENT

8½" (22 cm)

SKILL LEVEL

★ ☆ ☆ ☆ Easy

MATERIALS

2 silver-plated bead tips

4 silver-plated crimp beads

5 antique silver - (wire-wrapped) beads, 20 mm

1 antique silver - (wire-wrapped) bead, 16 mm

3 antique silver - (wire-wrapped) beads, 13 mm

1 square citrine bead, 15 mm

9" (23 cm) nylon-coated steel beading wire, 0.018" (0.45 mm)

2 antique silver jump rings, 5 mm

1 antique silver toggle clasp

TOOLS

2 chain-nose pliers

Crimping pliers

Wire cutters

INSTRUCTIONS

1 String 1 bead tip and 2 crimp beads onto the beading wire. Flatten the crimp beads and trim the excess wire. Fold the bead tip over the crimp beads.

2 String beads onto the beading wire in the following order: 2 x 13 mm wire-wrapped beads, 1 x 16 mm wire-wrapped bead, 3 x 20 mm wire-wrapped beads, 1 x citrine bead, 1 x 13 mm wire-wrapped bead, 2 x 20 mm wire-wrapped beads.

3 Repeat step 1 to finish the bracelet.

4 Open both jump rings and string each one onto a cord tip. Affix half the clasp onto each jump ring and close the jump rings. ©

Agate Ball and Silver Bead Cap Bracelet

THE BEAD CAPS IN THIS PROJECT ARE MADE FROM TIGHTLY WRAPPED WIRE. THEY ARE STRUNG IN PAIRS WITH THEIR WIDE SIDES TOGETHER, CREATING THE ILLUSION OF INDIVIDUAL WRAPPED BEADS.

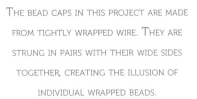

FINISHED MEASUREMENT

8½" (22 cm)

SKILL LEVEL

★ ☆ ☆ ☆ Easy

MATERIALS

2 silver-plated crimp beads

1 silver toggle clasp

10" (25 cm) nylon-coated steel beading wire, 0.018" (0.45 mm)

5 round textured agate beads, 16 mm

4 light silver wrapped wire bead caps, 16 mm

4 antique silver wrapped wire bead caps, 16 mm

TOOLS

Chain-nose pliers

Crimping pliers

Wire cutters

INSTRUCTIONS

1 String 2 crimp beads and half the clasp onto the beading wire. Tuck the end of the beading wire back into the crimp beads and flatten the crimp beads.

2 String beads onto the beading wire in the following order:
1 agate bead, 2 light silver bead caps (wide ends together),
1 agate bead, 2 dark silver bead caps (wide ends together),
1 agate bead, 2 light silver bead caps (wide ends together),
1 agate bead, 2 silver bead caps (wide ends together), 1 agate bead.

3 Measure the bracelet around your arm to make sure it is the right size. Add beads if necessary.

(CONTINUED ON PAGE 100)

(CONTINUED FROM PAGE 98)

4   String 2 crimp beads and the other half of the clasp onto the beading wire. Tuck the end of the beading wire back into the crimp beads and flatten the crimp beads. ◎

TIP IF POSSIBLE, MEASURE THE BRACELET AROUND THE WRIST OF THE PERSON WHO'LL BE WEARING IT BEFORE STRINGING ON THE SECOND PART OF THE CLASP. MAKE SURE THE BEADED WIRE IS FLEXIBLE ENOUGH TO WRAP COMFORTABLY AROUND THE WRIST.

Real Rainbow Bracelet

FINISHED MEASUREMENT

17½" (44 cm)

SKILL LEVEL

★ ★ ★ ☆ Advanced

THIS SPRIGHTLY BRACELET FEATURES EIGHT DIFFERENT COLORS OF SEED BEADS. YOU CAN ALSO USE JUST ONE OR TWO COLORS OF BEADS, OR LEAVE OUT THE BEADS ALTOGETHER AND WRAP THE MESH WITH WIRE AT REGULAR INTERVALS FOR A LIGHT, DELICATE DESIGN.

MATERIALS

18" (46 cm) white plastic mesh tube, 16 mm

2 gold-plated cord tips

27" (66 cm) gold-plated half-hard wire, 24-gauge (0.5 mm), cut into nine 3" (7.6 cm) pieces

8 teaspoons (approximately 600) seed beads, size 11°, in 8 different colors (turquoise, fuchsia, yellow, light pink, lime green, orange, dark green, dark orange)

2 gold-plated jump rings, 6 mm

1 gold-plated lobster claw clasp

1 gold-plated split ring, 8 mm

TOOLS

2 chain-nose pliers

1 teaspoon

INSTRUCTIONS

1   Insert one end of the mesh tube into a cord tip. Flatten the cord tip.

2 Wrap 1 piece of wire 10 times around the tube, about ¹/₈" (3 mm) from the flattened cord tip. Trim the tails of the wire and press the ends to flatten.

3 Insert 1 teaspoon of seed beads into the wire tube and allow the beads to settle above the wrapped wire.

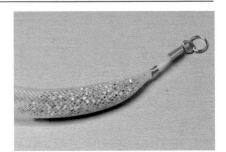

4 Tightly wrap 1 piece of wire about 10 times above the beads. Trim the tails and flatten the ends.

5 Repeat steps 3 and 4 until all the beads have been poured into the tube and secured with wire. Measure the bracelet as you work and adjust your use of the colors accordingly.

6 Trim the wire mesh past the last wrapped wire to ³/₈" (1 cm) and insert into a cord tip. Flatten the cord tip.

7 Open both jump rings and string one onto each cord tip. String the split ring onto one jump ring and the clasp onto the other jump ring. Close the jump rings. ©

TIP TO WEAR THIS BRACELET, WRAP IT TWICE AROUND YOUR WRIST. WRAP IT ONCE AROUND YOUR NECK FOR A TRENDY NECKLACE.

Crafty Crocheted Cuff

THIS CROCHETED PROJECT IS A BIT OF A CHALLENGE, BUT THE RESULT IS WORTH IT. THE AQUAMARINE BEADS ARE PERFECTLY SET OFF BY THE GOLD WIRE, MAKING FOR A DELICATE, ELEGANT DESIGN.

FINISHED MEASUREMENT

7½" (19 cm)

SKILL LEVEL

★ ★ ★ ☆ Advanced

MATERIALS

11 yd (10 m) gold-plated half-hard round wire, 28-gauge (0.3 mm)

110 aquamarine button beads, 4-5 mm

2 gold-filled lobster claw clasps

2 gold-filled jump rings

TOOLS

Crochet hook, #3

2 chain-nose pliers

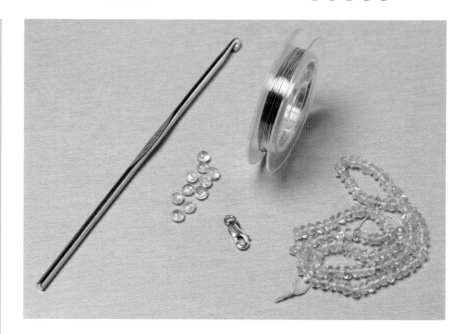

INSTRUCTIONS

1 String all the beads onto the wire.

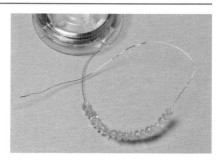

(CONTINUED ON PAGE 106)

(CONTINUED FROM PAGE 104)

2 Leave a 4" (10 cm) tail then single crochet 33 stitches, or until the bracelet is 16 cm long. Measure the chain around your wrist and add more stitches if necessary. Don't forget to leave room for the claps. Turn.

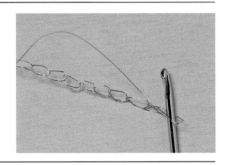

3 Double crochet each stitch in previous row, stringing a bead onto every 2nd stitch. Continue until the end of the chain. Turn.

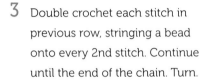

4 Repeat step 3 another 15 times, until bracelet is the desired width.

5 Pull the wire and wrap it a few times around the crocheted stitches to secure. Trim the excess.

6 Open the jump rings and string them through the top and bottom at one end of the bracelet. String a clasp onto each jump ring and close the jump rings. ◎

Golden Glass and Spiral Clasp Bracelet

FINISHED MEASUREMENT

7½" (19 cm)

SKILL LEVEL

★ ★ ★ ✦ Advanced

MATERIALS

Bracelet

3 square glass beads, transparent with gold leaf core, 10 x 10 mm

5 coin-shaped glass beads, transparent with gold leaf core, 10 mm

1 coin-shaped clear glass bead with gold leaf core, 20 mm

1 heart-shaped clear glass bead with gold leaf core, 10 mm

10 gold-plated eye pins, 1½" (4 cm)

8" (20 cm) gold-plated half-hard round wire, 20-gauge (0.8 mm), cut into two 4" (10 cm) pieces

TOOLS

Round-nose pliers

Chain-nose pliers

Wire cutters

Ring mandrel, or another tubular object with a ½" (13 mm) diameter

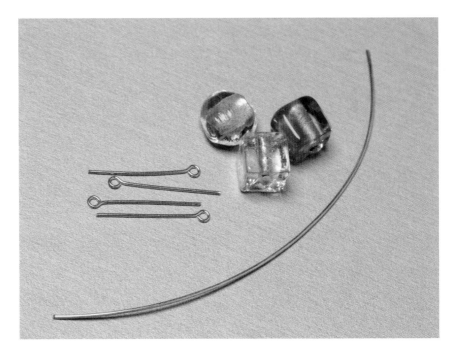

INSTRUCTIONS

1   String each bead onto an eye pin. Trim each eye pin to $^3/_8$" (1 cm) and make a loop but don't close it.

2 Connect the beads to each other using the open loop on each eye pin in the following order:
1 square bead, 2 small coin beads, 1 square bead, 1 small coin bead, 1 large coin bead, 1 heart bead, 1 small coin bead, 1 square bead, 1 small coin bead.

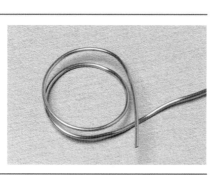

3 To make the round part of the clasp, wrap the middle of one piece of wire around a tubular object to form a ring with a $1/2$" (13 mm) diameter. Slip the wire off the object and wrap with one of the wires to secure.

4 Shape this end into a loop. Wrap the other end of wire a few times around the larger loop and trim the wire.

5 To make the straight part of the clasp, bend the other piece of wire in half and make a double loop at the bend.

6 Draw the two pieces of wire above the loop in opposite directions and twirl each side into a spiral. Make sure that the combined length of these spirals is long enough to be inserted into the round part of the clasp and hold the bracelet securely. ©

TIP MAKE SURE THAT THE SPIRAL PART OF THE CLASP CAN BE INSERTED EASILY INTO THE LOOP PART YET STILL KEEP THE BRACELET FIRMLY ON YOUR WRIST.

Triangle of Love Earrings

THIS ROMANTIC DESIGN TAKES A BIT OF PLANNING, BUT YOU'LL BE PLEASED WITH THE RESULT. I SELECTED A CHAIN THAT HAS LARGE AND SMALL LINKS SINCE I FOUND IT WAS JUST RIGHT FOR WEAVING IN THE WIRE.

FINISHED MEASUREMENT

1¾" (4.5 cm)

SKILL LEVEL

★ ★ ★ ☆ Advanced

MATERIALS

16" (40 cm) gold-filled half-hard round wire, 32-gauge (0.2 mm), cut into two 8" (20 cm) pieces

7" (18 cm) delicate gold-filled chain, cut into two 3½" (9 cm) pieces

50 white potato pearls, 2–2.5 mm

1 pair gold-filled ball ear posts, with loop

2 gold-filled jump rings, 3 mm

TOOLS

2 chain-nose pliers

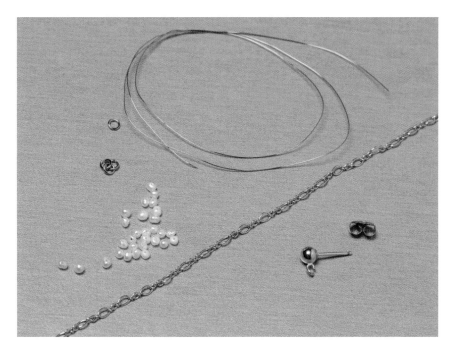

INSTRUCTIONS

1 Count the number of links in 1 piece of chain and divide this number into thirds. Place the chain on a piece of paper and mark these divisions on the paper with a pencil.

2 Leave the 1st third of the chain empty. Attach 1 piece of gold-filled wire to the first link in the second third of the chain by knotting the end of the wire securely to the link.

(CONTINUED ON PAGE 112)

(CONTINUED FROM PAGE 110)

3 String 5 pearls onto the wire and insert the wire into the next large link in the chain. Wrap the wire around that link and draw it out of the next link.

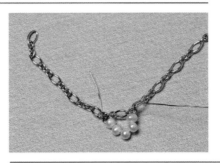

4 Repeat step 3 until you have strung pearls along the 2nd third of the earring.

5 Trim both ends of the wire. If the wire tips are still visible, gently press the wire against the links using pliers.

6 Open a jump ring and string both ends of the chain onto the jump ring. Orient the chain to form a triangle and position the beads along the outside bottom of the triangle (as shown at right). Close the jump ring.

7 Open the loop at the bottom of 1 ear post and connect it to the jump ring at the top of the triangle. Close the loop.

8 Repeat steps 1 to 7 to make the matching earring. ◎

Tip The chain I used for these earrings has both small and large links which is particularly conducive to dividing the chain into sections.

Pretty in Pink Pearl Earrings

HOOP EARRINGS ARE ALWAYS A FAVORITE. UPGRADE YOUR ORDINARY ONES TO SOMETHING PRETTY AND PEARLY.

FINISHED MEASUREMENT

3¼" (8 cm)

SKILL LEVEL

★ ★ ☆ ☆ Intermediate

MATERIALS

10 pink glass pearls, 8 mm

10 silver head pins, ⁴/₅" (2 cm)

2 white glass leaf beads, top-drilled, front-to-back, 20 mm

2½" (6 cm) silver-plated half-hard round wire, 24-gauge (0.5 mm), cut into two 1¼" (3 cm) pieces

2 thin jump rings, 5 mm

12" (30 cm) thin silver-plated chain, cut into six 2" (5 cm) pieces

1 pair of sterling silver hoop earrings, 3 cm

6 pink freshwater large-hole pearls, 5 mm

4 silver-plated leaf charms, 15 mm

2 white glass leaf beads, 10 mm

TOOLS

Chain-nose pliers

Round-nose pliers

Wire cutters

INSTRUCTIONS

1　String each pearl onto a head pin. Trim the wire to ³/₈" (1 cm) and make a closed loop.

2　String each 20 mm glass leaf bead onto a piece of wire. Draw the bead to the middle of the wire and twist one wire end around the other wire end 3 or 4 times. Make a loop with the wires.

3　Open both jump rings and string one end of 3 chain pieces onto each jump ring. Close the jump rings.

4　Open one hoop earring and string on the components in the following manner:
1 x 5 mm pearl, 1 x 8 mm pearl (on head pin), 2 x silver leaf charms (back to back),
1 x 5 mm pearl, 1 x 8 mm pearl (on head pin), 1 x 20 mm glass leaf bead, 1 x 5 mm pearl,
1 x jump ring with chains,
1 x 5 mm pearl, 1 x 8 mm pearl (on head pin), 2 x 10 mm glass leaf beads, 1 x pearl (on head pin).

5　Make a tiny bend at one end of the hoop earring and a small loop at the other end of the earring. Insert the bent end of the earring inside the loop to make sure that the earring closes securely.

6　Repeat steps 4 and 5 to make the matching earring. ©

Fluttering Dragonfly Earrings

These unusual earrings remind me of a delicate dragonfly wing. Replace the brown wire with any color you like.

FINISHED MEASUREMENT

2¼" (6 cm)

SKILL LEVEL

★ ★ ☆ ☆ Intermediate

MATERIALS

40" (101 cm) brown wire, 22-gauge (0.6 mm), cut into two 20" (50 cm) pieces

2 teardrop-shaped silver-plated connectors, 2" (5 cm) long, with interior and exterior top loops

2 silver-plated jump rings, 3 mm

2 silver-plated ball ear posts, with loop

TOOLS

2 chain-nose pliers

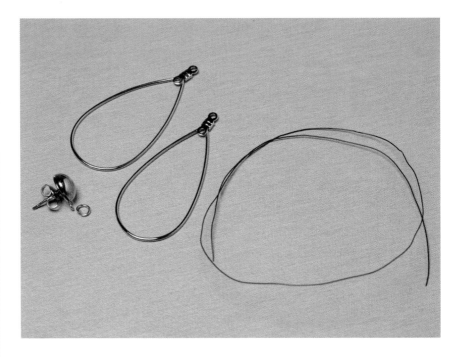

INSTRUCTIONS

1   Wrap the end of one piece of wire 3 or 4 times around the top of the connector, between the interior and exterior loop.

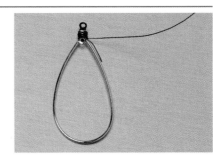

2   Bring the wire inside the connector and make a loop. Draw the end of the wire through the interior loop to secure the loop.

3   Make another loop inside the connector and secure it in the interior loop. Repeat to make a total of 5 loops of varying sizes. Bring the end of the wire back up through the connector and wrap it between the two loops at the top.

4   Conceal the tip of the wire by pressing it firmly onto the connector.

5   Open a jump ring and string it through the loop at the top of the connector and the loop at the bottom of the ear post. Close the loop.

6   Repeat steps 1 to 5 to make the matching earring. ©

Lovely Link Earrings

FOLLOW THESE SIMPLE STEPS TO MAKE A PRETTY PAIR OF DANGLY EARRINGS WITH LEFTOVER LINKS FROM THE GRACIOUSLY GOLD PEARL CLUSTER NECKLACE (PAGES 51 TO 53).

FINISHED MEASUREMENT

3" (7.6 cm)

SKILL LEVEL

★ ☆ ☆ ☆ Easy

MATERIALS

1 pair gold-plated ear wires

5" (12 cm) gold-plated large-link chain, cut into two 2¹/₂" (6 cm) pieces

TOOLS

Flat-nose pliers

Round-nose pliers

INSTRUCTIONS

1   String each pearl cluster onto an eye pin. Trim each eye pin to ³/₈" (1 cm) and make a closed loop.

2   String the link at one end of one chain onto the loop. Close the loop.

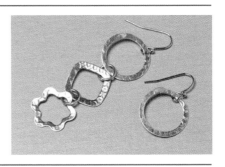

3   Repeat steps 1 and 2 to make the matching earring. ◎

Creative Wire Jewelry

Sparkling Spiral Earrings

THESE EARRINGS ARE A SIMPLE YET LOVELY COMPLEMENT TO THE SPARKLING SILVER SPIRAL BRACELET (PAGES 93 TO 95)

FINISHED MEASUREMENT

2½" (6 cm)

SKILL LEVEL

★ ☆ ☆ ☆   Easy

MATERIALS

2 flat rectangular agate beads, 20 x 15 x 5 mm

2 sterling silver eye pins, 2" (5 cm)

4" (10 cm) sterling silver half-hard round wire, 18-gauge (1 mm), cut into two 2" (5 cm) pieces

1 pair sterling silver ear wires

TOOLS

Round-nose pliers

Wire cutters

INSTRUCTIONS

1   String an agate bead onto an eye pin. Trim the eye pin to $^3/_8$" (1 cm) and make a closed loop.

2   Twist 1 piece of wire into a spiral shape with a $^3/_8$" (1 cm) straight end. Shape the end into a loop.

3   String the loop on the spiral onto the bottom loop of the agate bead. Close the loop.

4   String the top loop of the agate bead onto an ear wire.

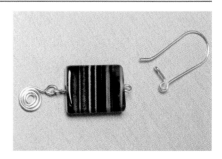

5   Repeat steps 1 to 4 to make the matching earring. ◎

Dangling Flower Earrings

THESE PRETTY EARRINGS, MAKE A BIG IMPRESSION. A GREAT PROJECT FOR PRACTICING YOUR FLOWER-MAKING SKILLS, THEY CAN BE WORN WITH THE GOLDEN BOUQUET NECKLACE (PAGES 62 TO 65).

FINISHED MEASUREMENT

3" (7.6 cm)

SKILL LEVEL

★ ★ ★ ☆ Advanced

MATERIALS

8" (20 cm) gold-plated or gold-filled half-hard round wire, 20-gauge (0.8 mm)

1 pair gold-plated leverback ear wires

3¼" (8 cm) gold-plated small-link chain, cut into two 1½" (4 cm) pieces

TOOLS

Round-nose pliers

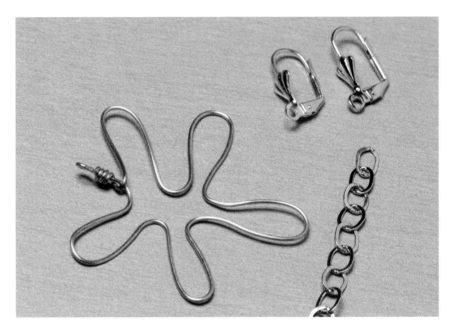

(CONTINUED ON PAGE 122)

(CONTINUED FROM PAGE 120)

INSTRUCTIONS

1   Gently bend 1 piece of wire near the middle, using pliers or your hands, to make 2 rounded petals. Continue bending the wire to make 5 rounded petal shapes.

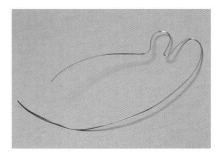

2   Bring the wire ends together. Wrap one end around the other end a few times; then bend the wrapped end into a loop. Don't close the loop.

3   Connect the link at one end of one piece of chain to the loop in the flower. Close the loop.

4   Open the loop at the bottom of 1 ear wire and string it through the link at the other end of the chain. Close the loop.

5   Repeat steps 1 to 4 to make the matching earring. ◎

Elegant Egyptian Earrings

FINISHED MEASUREMENT

1¾" (4.5 cm)

SKILL LEVEL

★ ★ ★ ☆ Advanced

MATERIALS

16" (40 cm) gold-plated or gold-filled half-hard wire, 20-gauge (0.8 mm), cut into two 8" (20 cm) pieces

24" (60 cm) gold-plated or gold-filled half-hard wire, 24-gauge (0.5 mm), cut into two 12" (30 cm) pieces

2 teardrop turquoise beads, middle-drilled, top-to-bottom, 12 x 7 mm

2 gold-filled jump rings, 3 mm

1 pair gold-plated ear wires

TOOLS

Tubular object with a 1²/₅" (3.5 cm) diameter

Chain-nose pliers

Round-nose pliers

Wire cutters

INSTRUCTIONS

1 Wrap 1 piece of 20-gauge (0.8 mm) wire halfway around a round object with a 3.5 cm diameter in order to shape the wire into a half-circle with this diameter.

2 Measure ⁴/₅" (2 cm) from the middle of the half-circle shape on either side of the wire and fold the wire inwards on each side.

3 Bring the wires together directly above the center of the half-circle. Bend both wires upwards at a 90-degree angle.

4 Measure ¹/₂" (1.3 cm) upwards along one wire. Trim the wire and make a small loop at the tip.

5 Wrap the other wire around this wire, in the area between the bend you made in step 3 and the loop you made in step 4. Trim excess wire if necessary.

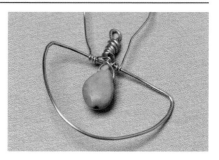

6 String 1 turquoise bead onto 1 piece of 24-gauge (0.5 mm) wire and draw it along to the middle of the wire.

7 Bring the ends of the wire together and wrap together 3 or 4 times to secure the bead in place. Wrap as close to the turquoise bead as possible using the pliers.

8 Bring the turquoise bead to the middle of the half-circle you completed in step 5. Wrap one of the wires extending from the top of the bead around the rightmost horizontal wire in the half circle. Wrap the wire tightly along this wire until you reach the right side of the horizontal wire (the top of the half circle). Trim the wire.

9 Wrap the other wire extending from the top of the bead around the leftmost horizontal wire in the half circle. When you reach the left side of the wire (the top of the half circle), trim the wire.

10 Open the loop at the bottom of 1 ear wire and string it through the loop at the top of the half-circle. Close the loop.

11 Repeat steps 1 to 10 to make the matching earring. ◎

Twinkling Turquoise Earrings

WITH TWISTED GOLD WIRE AND COLORED BEADS, THESE EARRINGS ARE BRIGHT AND VIVACIOUS.

FINISHED MEASUREMENT

1¼ (3 cm)

SKILL LEVEL

★ ★ ★ ☆ Advanced

MATERIALS

10" (24 cm) gold-plated or gold-filled half-hard round wire, 20-gauge (0.8 mm), cut into two 5" (12 cm) pieces

10" (24 cm) gold-plated or gold-filled half-hard round wire, 24-gauge (0.5 mm), cut into two 5" (12 cm) pieces

16" (40 cm) gold-plated or gold-filled half-hard round wire, 24-gauge (0.5 mm), cut into two 8" (20 cm) pieces

38 round turquoise beads, 2 mm

4 green button beads, 4 mm

2 red button coral beads, 4 mm

6 gold-filled jump rings, 5 mm

1 pair gold-filled ball ear posts, with loop

TOOLS

Small rolling pin (optional)

Flat-nose pliers

Wire cutters

Round-nose pliers

Creative Wire Jewelry

(CONTINUED ON PAGE 128)

(CONTINUED FROM PAGE 126)

INSTRUCTIONS

1 Wrap 1 piece of 20-gauge (0.8 mm) wire halfway around a small rolling pin or your finger to shape it into a half-circle.

2 Measure $^4/_5$" (2 cm) from the middle of the half-circle on one side of the wire and make an outward loop in the wire. Bring the wire end towards the middle of the half-circle; then fold the wire upwards at a 90-degree angle.

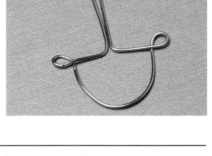

3 Repeat step 2 with the other side of the wire.

4 Twist one wire end 3 or 4 times around the other wire end to secure the shape. Trim the straight end of wire to $^3/_8$" (1 cm) and make a loop.

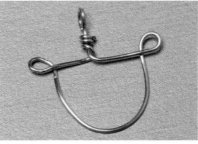

5 String 1 green bead, 1 coral bead and 1 green bead onto one 8" (20 cm) piece of 24-gauge (0.5 mm) wire. Draw the beads to the middle of the wire. Twist the wires together 3 or 4 times just above the beads to secure the beads.

6 Place these beads below the loop you made in step 4. Wrap each of the wires extending from the top of the beads around one of the horizontal wires in the shape. Trim excess wire.

7 Twist the end of one 5" (12 cm) piece of 20-gauge (0.8 mm) wire into a small spiral. Make sure you can fit an open jump ring into the middle of the spiral.

8 String 19 turquoise beads onto the wire; then twist a spiral at the other end of the wire.

9 Open a jump ring and string it through one of the loops you formed in step 2 and the spiral you made in step 7. Close the jump ring.

10 Open a jump ring and string it through the other loop from step 3 and the spiral you made in step 8. Close the jump ring.

11 Open a jump ring and string it through the loop at the top of the earring and the loop in the ear post. Close the jump ring.

12 Repeat steps 1 to 11 to make the matching earring. ◎

Beaded Bounty Hair Combs

DRESS UP YOUR HAIRSTYLE WITH EASE WITH
ONE OR TWO OF THESE BEAUTIFUL ACCESSORIES.
TRY DIFFERENT COMBINATIONS OF BEAD COLORS
AND SHAPES. FOR A SOFTER LOOK, INTEGRATE A
FEW PIECES OF COLORFUL RIBBON.

FINISHED MEASUREMENT

3¼" (8 cm)

SKILL LEVEL

★ ☆ ☆ ☆ Easy

MATERIALS

1 brass hair comb, 3" (7.6 cm)

12" (30.5 cm) silver-plated
half-hard round wire,
24-gauge (0.5 mm)

About 40 small glass beads,
in various shapes and sizes

TOOLS

Wire cutters

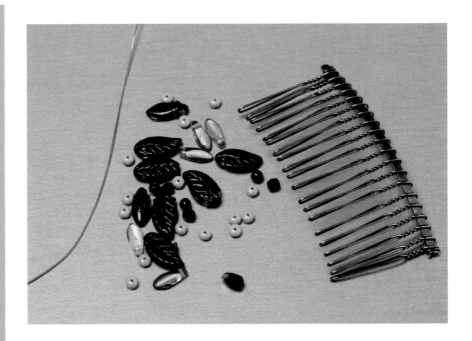

INSTRUCTIONS

1   Wrap one end the wire several
times around one end of the
hair comb base until the wire is
securely attached.

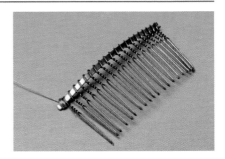

2   String a few beads onto the
    wire and draw them along until
    they are flush with the hair
    comb base.

3   Wrap the wire around the base
    between two comb teeth.

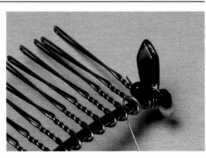

4   Repeat steps 2 and 3 until you
    reach the other end of the comb.
    Wrap the wire several times
    around this end to secure the
    beads in place. Tie a knot in the
    wire to secure it; then cut the
    end. Tuck in the end of the wire
    using pliers. ©

Spiral Posy Ring

THE TECHNIQUE USED FOR THIS RING CAN ALSO BE USED TO MAKE A BROOCH OR PENDANT. MAKE TWO IDENTICAL SPIRALS AND STRING THEM ONTO EAR WIRES FOR A BEAUTIFUL PAIR OF EARRINGS!

FINISHED MEASUREMENT

¾" (2 cm) diameter

SKILL LEVEL

★ ★ ☆ ☆ Intermediate

MATERIALS

40" (100 cm) gold-plated half-hard round wire, 24-gauge (0.5 mm), cut into ten 4" (10 cm) pieces

1 silver-plated adjustable ring base with 10 loops

TOOLS

Wire cutters

Round-nose pliers

Chain-nose pliers

Jeweler's hammer and block

INSTRUCTIONS

1 Twist 1 piece of wire into a tight spiral with a ³/₈" (1 cm) diameter. Make a loop at the straight end of the wire but don't close the loop.

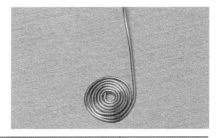

2 Place the spiral on the block and strike it with the flat side of the hammer head to flatten.

3 String the loop on the spiral through a loop in the ring base. Close the loop.

4 Repeat steps 1 to 3 another 9 times to complete the ring. ☺

Blossom Bud Ring

THIS EYE-CATCHING RING CHIMES
DELICATELY WHEN YOU MOVE YOUR HAND.
BE SURE TO CHOOSE A HIGH-QUALITY RING
BASE BECAUSE THIS IS ONE DESIGN YOU'LL
WANT TO WEAR OFTEN.

FINISHED MEASUREMENT

¾" (2 cm) diameter

SKILL LEVEL

★ ★ ☆ ☆ Intermediate

MATERIALS

5 gold-plated head pins,
2" (5 cm)

5 folding two-sided gold-plated bead caps

5 rose opal bicone crystal beads, 4 mm

5 pink silver-cored glass foil beads, 10 mm

1 gold-plated ring base with 1 loop

TOOLS

Wire cutters

2 chain-nose pliers

Round-nose pliers

INSTRUCTIONS

1   String 1 crystal bead, 1 glass foil bead and 1 bead cap onto a head pin. Partially fold the bead cap over the foil bead. Make sure the bead is still visible in the bead cap. Trim the wire to ¹/₂" (13 mm). Make a loop in the wire that is large enough to fit through the loop in the ring base. Don't close the loop.

2   Repeat step 1 another 4 times.

3   String the open loop of a decorated head pin through the loop in the ring base. Close the loop.

4   Repeat step 2 to attach the rest of the head pins to the ring base. If there is no room in the ring base for the 5th head pin, attach it to the loop on one of the other head pins. ◎

Lucky Leaf Ring

IF YOU LIKE WEARING MATCHING PIECES OF JEWELRY, YOU'LL LOVE THIS TECHNIQUE. SIMPLY CHOOSE A BEAD OR CHARM THAT APPEARS IN THE NECKLACE OR BRACELET YOU WANT TO WEAR AND MAKE A MATCHING RING.

FINISHED MEASUREMENT

³/₄" (2 cm) diameter

SKILL LEVEL

★ ★ ☆ ☆ Intermediate

MATERIALS

1 pewter leaf charm, 30 mm

8" (30 cm) silver-plated half-hard round wire, 20-gauge (0.8 mm)

TOOLS

Wire cutters

Ring mandrel

INSTRUCTIONS

1 String the charm onto the wire and draw it to the middle of the wire. Twist the two ends of wire together above the charm to secure it in place.

2 Wrap the wires around the ring mandrel at the desired diameter for 3 full revolutions.

3 Slip the wire loops off the mandrel and twist them together. Trim the excess wire and tuck in the ends. ◎

Rock Candy Ring

ONE VERY SPECIAL GEMSTONE: THAT'S REALLY ALL YOU NEED TO MAKE THIS IMPRESSIVE RING. ITS STRIKING APPEARANCE BELIES ITS RELATIVELY EASY CONSTRUCTION.

FINISHED MEASUREMENT

¾" (2 cm) diameter

SKILL LEVEL

★ ★ ☆ ☆ Intermediate

MATERIALS

1 oval transparent blue gemstone, middle-drilled, top-to-bottom, 25 x 15 mm

20" (51 cm) gold-plated half-hard round wire, 24-gauge (0.5 mm)

TOOLS

Chain-nose pliers

Wire cutters

Ring mandrel

INSTRUCTIONS

1   String the gemstone onto the wire and draw it to the middle of the wire. Wrap the wires together several times above the gemstone.

2   Place the gemstone on a ring mandrel and wrap the wires several times around the mandrel at the desired diameter.

3   When you have about 1¹⁄₄" (3 cm) of free wire left, remove the ring from the mandrel and wrap the ends several times around the wire just below the gemstone. Tighten the wrap using pliers. ©

Pearly Flower Power Brooch

THE NEXT THREE PROJECTS DEMONSTRATE HOW WIRE CAN BE USED TO MAKE SIMPLE AND DISTINCT BROOCHES. THIS FIRST DESIGN INCLUDES A PIECE OF SHELL, A HANDFUL OF FRESHWATER PEARLS, AND A PIN BACK. IN THE FOLLOWING TWO PROJECTS, YOU'LL USE WIRE TO MAKE THE POINTED PIN AS WELL.

FINISHED MEASUREMENT

5¼" (13 cm) diameter

SKILL LEVEL

★ ★ ☆ ☆ Intermediate

MATERIALS

Sketching materials and/or inexpensive wire

20" (50 cm) silver-plated half-hard round wire, 16-gauge (1.3 mm)

12" (30 cm) silver-plated half-hard round wire, 24-gauge (0.5 mm)

7 flat white freshwater pearls, 13 mm

1 round shell, 3 cm

1 silver-plated pin back

TOOLS

Chain-nose pliers

Round-nose pliers

INSTRUCTIONS

1 Draw a sketch of a 6-petal flower and/or practice making the flower with inexpensive wire. Shape the 16-gauge (1.3 mm) wire into a flower using your fingers and pliers.

2 Twist the ends of the wire together to secure the shape.

3 Secure the 24-gauge (0.5 mm) wire to the flower by twisting one end of the wire a few times around the inner area of a flower petal.

4 String 1 pearl onto the wire and position it at the base of a petal.

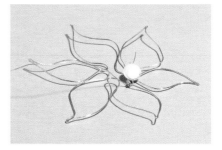

(CONTINUED ON PAGE 142)

(CONTINUED FROM PAGE 140)

5 Draw the wire over to the next petal and wrap it around the inner area of the petal a few times. String 1 pearl onto the wire and position it as desired.

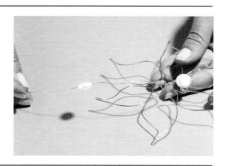

6 Repeat step 5 another 5 times until all the pearls have been secured in place around the center of the flower. Twist the thin wire securely and trim the excess.

7 Turn over the flower and affix the shell to the back of the pearls. Affix the pin back to the back of the shell. ©

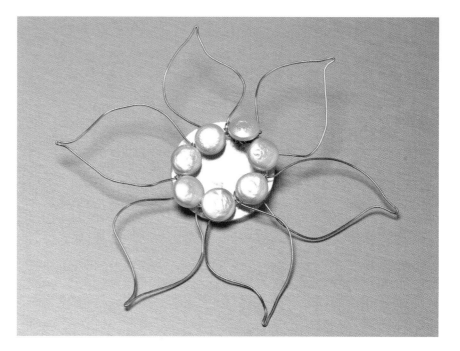

TIP FOR A VINTAGE LOOK, YOU CAN SUBSTITUTE THE SHELL WITH A PIECE OF WHITE TULLE FABRIC AT THE BACK OF THE PIN.

Creative Wire Jewelry

Heart-on-Your-Sleeve Brooch

PRACTICE THIS SIMPLE DESIGN WITH INEXPENSIVE WIRE FIRST. WEAR IT WITH A KNIT SWEATER OR VEST SO THAT THE PIN DOESN'T DAMAGE THE FABRIC.

FINISHED MEASUREMENT

2¾" (7 cm) diameter

SKILL LEVEL

★ ★ ☆ ☆　Intermediate

MATERIALS

Sketching materials and/or inexpensive wire

18" (46 cm) sterling silver half-hard round wire, 14-gauge (1.5 mm)

TOOLS

Jeweler's hammer and block

Round-nose pliers

Chain-nose pliers

INSTRUCTIONS

1　Draw a sketch of a heart and/or practice making one with inexpensive wire.

2　Measure 4" (10 cm) from one end of the wire and bend it to shape the bottom of the heart.

3　Make a loop at the tip of the short side of the wire but don't close the loop.

4　Using your sketch as a guide, shape the longer side of wire into a heart. Insert the wire into the loop from step 3 and close the loop. Continue shaping the rest of the wire into a half-circle that forms an arc over the top of the heart.

5　Tap the end of the wire with the flat face of the hammer. ◎

INDEX